P9-BUH-331

Charles H. Goren's
New Contract Bridge
in a Nutshell

Charles H. Goren's
New Contract Bridge
in a Nutshell

by *Charles H. Goren*

Doubleday & Company, Inc.
Garden City, New York
1959

FOREWORD

With this new presentation of CONTRACT BRIDGE IN A NUTSHELL a word of explanation is in order.

In the early days of contract bridge, the annual change of design was as regular a procedure as that which is observed in the motorcar industry. When a few years later I entered the field of writing I declined to fall into this pattern and thus avoided the charge usually leveled against other writers, to the effect that changes in the system were devised primarily for the purpose of stimulating sales. However, in 1949 I presented the first revolutionary change when I introduced my own variety of Point Count for suit bidding, which has since become universally accepted.

Success bred in me a certain indolence and I was content to drift along for some years without making any further drastic recommendations.

But the public at times grows restless. So at its instance in 1957 I sacrificed the leisure to which I had looked forward in order to produce GOREN'S NEW

CONTRACT BRIDGE COMPLETE. The changes therein recommended were first presented by *Sports Illustrated* magazine in an article entitled by them "My Ten New Commandments." The book's reception has been most gratifying and it has since become the most successful book in the history of bridge.

CONTRACT BRIDGE IN A NUTSHELL has always, I am happy and grateful to say, been an extremely popular adjunct to CONTRACT BRIDGE COMPLETE, presenting as it does in this condensed and easily usable form the essence of all the important points in bridge tips and instruction. It is necessary now, therefore, to bring out this new edition in a revised format, completely up to date, to preserve and enhance its value as a compendium of basic instruction.

I have added some new elements that were not before in CONTRACT BRIDGE IN A NUTSHELL and dropped others that have ceased to be of importance in the modern game. It has been revised in other respects and in format to make it even more useful and handy for the bridge player who wants the necessary information, streamlined down to an easily accessible handbook.

For the most complete instruction and reference material I suggest the reader continue to peruse GOREN'S NEW CONTRACT BRIDGE COMPLETE.

Once again I should like to offer my gratitude to the millions of bridge players throughout the world for their devotion to the game. May it continue to bring you the pleasure that I share with you.

Charles H. Goren

Charles H. Goren's
New Contract Bridge
in a Nutshell

VALUATION TABLES

Ace	4 points
King	3 points
Queen	2 points
Jack	1 point

The pack contains 40 points.
An average hand contains 10 points.

Unprotected honors: Honor cards other than the Ace have their value impaired when they are not protected. When the King is alone, its value should be reduced from 3 to 2 points, and the Queen from 2 points to 1. A lone Jack should not be assigned any high-card value. Similarly, the Queen or the Jack, if it is accompanied by only one small card, is not sufficiently protected and should be reduced by a point. Consequently the Queen becomes worth 1 point and the Jack loses its value almost entirely.

Add one point if your hand contains all four Aces.

11

Deduct one point if your hand is Aceless.

In valuing a hand for purposes of No Trump, only high cards receive our attention. But for purposes of suit bidding, distributional values must be taken into account. For purposes of computing the value of a hand at a suit bid, the high-card values must be added to the distributional values.

TABLE OF DISTRIBUTION POINTS

Add 3 points if your hand contains a void.
Add 2 points if your hand contains a singleton.
Add 1 point for each doubleton.[1]

Since minimum hands must contain at least two defensive (quick) tricks, I include a table of such defensive tricks:

2 Quick Tricks	1½ Quick Tricks
A K	A Q
1 Quick Trick	½ Quick Trick
A	K x
K Q	

Some players have fallen into the erroneous belief that the distributional points which I allow in the opening hand are ruffing values. Nothing could be farther from the truth. The values for voids, singletons, and doubletons are not ruffing values but pattern points. What I am really doing is allowing

[1]This is the distributional count for declarer's hand; that is, when you are naming your own suit. It is not to be confused with the distributional count for dummy hands; that is, when a raise is offered to partner. This will be found on pages 34–35.

12

points for long cards. For every short suit there must be a correspondingly long card. If you are scientifically interested in the development of this count, you may like to read the following. If not, it is suggested that you skip it.

A	B
♠ A x x	♠ A x x
♡ A K J x x	♡ A K J x x x
◇ x x x	◇ x x x
♣ x x	♣ x

Hand A is worth 13 points, 12 in high cards and 1 for the doubleton. We could just as well say 12 in high cards and 1 for the fifth Heart. Similarly, Hand B is worth 14 points, 12 in high cards and 2 for the singleton. Here, too, we could express it as 12 in high cards and one for the fifth Heart and one for the sixth. Whenever there is a singleton there must be two long cards; whenever there is a doubleton there must be one long card.

If the net result is the same, why have I chosen to count short suits rather than long cards? It is a matter of pedagogy. The student finds it easier to keep track of his long cards in this manner.

What is a long card? In the trump suit, long cards start at the fifth card. In a side suit, the fourth card is considered a long card. The rule might therefore be stated that the true value of a hand is computed by counting the high cards and adding a point each for the fifth and sixth cards of the trump suit and one point for the fourth card (also the fifth) of any side suit. This would be very cumbersome; so cum-

13

bersome, in fact, that some writers were induced to forget about the fourth card of the side suits and therefore arrived at a false evaluation of unbalanced hands.

To illustrate:

	C		D
♠	A x x	♠	A x x x
♡	A K J x x	♡	A K J x x
◇	x x x	◇	x x
♣	x x	♣	x x

Obviously D is a better hand than C. It has better distribution. If we counted only the fifth Heart, both hands would have the same value of 13 points. Actually D is worth 14 points. It was so much simpler to add 1 point for each doubleton to arrive at the true value.

Similarly, where the distribution is 4-4-4-1, the hand contains two long cards and therefore 2 distributional points. Remember that the trump suit is not counted until the fifth card is reached. Inasmuch as the suggested trump suit will have no fifth card, your long cards consist of the fourth of each of the side suits. If this were not so, and if only the fifth card were counted, then we would reach the conclusion that the following two hands would have the same value, which is obviously false.

♠	A x x x	♠	A 10 x x
♡	A x x	♡	A x x x
◇	A x x	◇	x
♣	x x x	♣	A x x x

But this is all a matter of pedagogy, and if you

14

don't like to count short suits, then you may do it this way with the same results: Start counting your trump suit at the fifth card, allowing one for that card and any subsequent one, and count your side suits by adding one for the fourth card of any side suit and also one for the fifth if you happen to have a second five-card suit. It is all a matter of taste.

BIDDABLE SUITS

A *biddable* suit is one which may be bid, provided the hand itself calls for a bid. A biddable suit must contain at least four cards, and for purposes of opening the bidding in a major suit you must have at least four high-card points.

These suits are biddable:

| KJxx | Axxx | QJ10x[1] |

Naturally such suits may not be rebid unless partner makes a jump raise in them.

A rebiddable suit is a good suit of five or more cards, strong enough to be bid a second time (provided the hand calls for it) without support from partner in that suit.

These suits are rebiddable:

| AKxxx | AJxxx | QJ9xx |
| KQxxx | 10xxxxx | |

Suits that are stronger than these may be bid *three* times without support from partner, provided the hand itself is strong enough to justify such action.

---

[1]The addition of the 10 makes this combination eligible.

OPENING BIDS

OPENING BIDS OF ONE IN A SUIT

The value of a hand for purposes of opening the bidding is computed by adding the high-card points to the distributional points.

THE REQUIREMENTS

If your hand contains 13 points, you have an optional opening. You should open it if you anticipate no discomfort on the rebid.

If your hand contains 14 points, it must be opened. For example:

♠ AKJx   ♡ xxx   ◊ Axx   ♣ xxx

Pass. This hand is worth only 12 points.

♠ AKxx   ♡ AJxx   ◊ xx   ♣ xxx

Bid one Spade. The hand counts 13 points. The option to open should be exercised because you have a convenient rebid of two Hearts if partner should respond with two Diamonds or two Clubs.

In third position, after two passes, you may open with 10 or 11 points, if you have a reasonably good suit.

♠ A K J x x   ♡ J x   ◊ x x x   ♣ x x x

In third position open one Spade, but take no further action.

THE SHORT CLUB BID

This is not a system or convention. It is a device for the convenience of the opening bidder when a hand must be opened and there is no *convenient* opening bid.

♠ Q 10 x x   ♡ K x x x   ◊ J x   ♣ A K x

This hand counts to 14 points and is therefore a mandatory opening. However, it would be improper to open with 1 Spade because neither major suit is biddable. It is necessary, therefore, to open with 1 Club.

Don't ask partner: "Do you use the short Club?" That should be treated as strictly his personal affair. It's none of your business, except that you ought not to raise a Club bid without four good Clubs in your own hand. Another illustration:

♠ A K x x   ♡ J 10 x   ◊ x x x   ♣ A Q x

This hand, containing 14 points, should not be passed. If you open with one Spade, what will you do when partner responds two Diamonds? The answer is, *squirm*. If, for your own convenience, you open with one Club, partner is able to respond with *one* Diamond or *one* Heart, whereupon you rebid one Spade. Any hand counting 14 points must be opened, since it is an Ace above average. For example:

♠ A J x   ♡ J 10 x   ◇ K x x   ♣ K Q x x

A mandatory opening of one Club.

Hands counting 13 may be opened if they contain a convenient rebid.

CHOICE OF SUITS TO BID FIRST

With two five-card biddable suits bid first the higher ranking (not necessarily the stronger).

With two suits, one five and the other four, bid the longer suit first (with certain exceptions).

With two suits, 6–5, bid the longer suit first. Then bid the five-card suit twice.

With two suits, 6–4, bid the long suit twice before showing the four-card suit, unless the latter is a major suit and can be shown at the level of one.

For example:

♠ A Q 10 x   ♡ x   ◇ A Q J x x x   ♣ x x

OPENER	RESPONDER
1 ◇	1 ♡
1 ♠	

19

With 6–5 distribution: Opener holds

♠ x ♡ AKxxx ◇ AQJxxx ♣ x

OPENER	RESPONDER
1 ◇	1 ♠
2 ♡	2 ♠
3 ♡	

The rebid of three Hearts shows a five-card Heart suit and therefore implies a six-card Diamond suit, since if they were of the same length Hearts would have been bid first.

Exception to 5–4 distribution:

♠ AQJx ♡ KQxxx ◇ xx ♣ xx

An opening bid of one Spade is recommended in order to make your rebid easier.

On this hand, if you should open with one Heart and partner responds two Diamonds, a two Spade rebid by you would force partner to three Hearts if he simply wished to return to your first suit. This gets rather expensive.

To put the exception in the form of a rule:

On hands of moderate strength with a five-card suit and a four-card suit which are next-door neighbors (Spades and Hearts, Hearts and Diamonds, or Diamonds and Clubs), if the higher ranking suit is a good four-card suit, *treat the lower-ranking five-card suit as though it were really the same length as the other.*

In other words, when your second bid is made at such a level that it becomes impossible for your partner to return to two of your first suit, *you must have a very good hand*.

NOTE: Treat any very weak five-card suit as though it were a four-card suit.

CHOICE BETWEEN FOUR-CARD SUITS

Look for the shortest suit in your hand (either singleton or doubleton) and bid first that suit which ranks below your singleton or doubleton. If the suit below is not biddable, select the next below that. A slight exception is suggested in cases where you hold four Hearts and four Clubs. An opening bid of one Club is recommended in that case, regardless of the shortest suit.

♠ xxx	♡ xx	◇ AKxx	♣ AQJx	1 Diamond
♠ AKxx	♡ xxx	◇ xx	♣ AQJx	1 Club
♠ AKxx	♡ KQJx	◇ xxx	♣ xx	1 Spade
♠ xxx	♡ AKxx	◇ AQJx	♣ xx	1 Heart
♠ AQxx	♡ Jxx	◇ AKxx	♣ xx	1 Spade
♠ AQxx	♡ xx	◇ AKxx	♣ Jxx	1 Diamond
♠ AKxx	♡ AJ10x	◇ x	♣ KJxx	1 Club

Exception:

♠ AKJx   ♡ AQxx   ◇ KQJx   ♣ x

Holding about 20 points, where the normal bid would be one Spade, open with one Diamond instead to make it easier for partner to respond.

21

OPENING PRE-EMPTIVE BIDS

A pre-emptive bid is an opening of three, four, or five in a suit. It shows a hand that is poor in honor tricks but long in trumps. The purpose is to make it difficult for the opponents to get together.

Don't open with a pre-emptive bid merely because you have a long suit. A hand containing 11 or more points in high cards should not be opened with a pre-emptive bid.

In making a pre-emptive bid, you should be reasonably sure that if doubled you will not be set more than 500 points. This means you may bid for two tricks more than you can actually win in your own hand when vulnerable; and three tricks more when not vulnerable.

♠ K Q J x x x x x   ♡ x   ◇ x x   ♣ x x

Bid four Spades not vulnerable; three Spades, vulnerable.

Don't raise your partner's pre-emptive bids unless you have an unusual amount of strength. You know approximately how many tricks he can win. You ought to be quite sure you can win the rest.

Don't rescue partner's pre-emptive bids. Remember his hand is good only in his own suit and it's not much good even there.

Slam tries after a pre-emptive bid rarely pay.

Don't double opponent if you are counting on partner to produce a defensive trick where he has pre-empted.

OPENING BIDS OF TWO IN A SUIT

An opening bid of two in a suit is absolutely forcing to game. That means that BOTH partners are unconditionally obligated to keep bidding until a final game contract is reached. The only excuse other than sudden death for failure to reach game is that the opponents have in the meantime been doubled.

Such an opening two-bid should therefore show virtually a game in hand, to allow for the case in which partner holds a bust.

The high-card requirement for an opening demand bid is at least four quick tricks.

Here is a foolproof formula setting forth the requirements for the opening bid of two in a suit.

A. With a good five-card major suit—25 points.
B. With a good six-card major suit—23 points.
C. With a good seven-card major suit—21 points.
D. With a second good five-card suit, 1 point less than above. Where you have a good major two-suiter, you may relax the requirements by as many as 2 points.
E. If it appears that the hand must play in a minor suit, the requirements should be increased by 2 points.

For example:

♠ A K x x ♡ A K x x ◇ x ♣ A K x x

Bid one Club. This hand is worth only 23 points.

♠ A K Q J x x x ♡ A x x ◇ A x ♣ x

Bid two Spades. You have 21 points and a good seven-card suit (only four losers).

♠ A K J 9 x x ♡ A Q 10 ◇ x x ♣ A K

23

Bid two Spades. You have 23 points and a good six-card suit.

♠ A Q x x x　♡ A K x　◇ A K x　♣ x x

Bid one Spade. This hand is worth only 21 points.

♠ K Q J x x x　♡ A Q J x x x　◇ x　♣ None

Bid one Spade. You have game in hand but not four quick tricks.

RESPONSES TO TWO-BIDS

If your partner opens with two of a suit, you are not merely forced to respond once, but you must keep bidding until a *final game contract* is reached (or the opponents have been doubled in the meantime)—and that regardless of how hopeless your hand may be.

With a weak hand the conventional response is two No Trump, regardless of your distribution.

But where specific values are held:

First make a natural response. Then after the trump suit has been established, the partnership shows each Ace and King individually.

The natural response may take the form of a simple raise (this response requires normal trump support), a simple suit takeout, or a response of three No Trump. If your hand contains one quick trick, you may make a positive response with 7 points. But if your hand contains only ½ quick trick, you need 8 points for a positive response.

If you choose to make your response in another suit, that suit should be at least five to the Q J.

24

Partner opens with two Hearts.

A. ♠ x   ♡ 10 x x x x x   ◊ x x x   ♣ x x x
Two No Trump.

B. ♠ x x   ♡ Q x x x   ◊ K Q x   ♣ x x x x
Three Hearts. Normal trump support and 9 points.

C. ♠ K J x x x   ♡ x x x   ◊ K x x   ♣ x x
Two Spades. Natural response with 7 high-card points
and 1 quick trick.

D. ♠ x x   ♡ Q x x   ◊ K Q x   ♣ J x x x x
Three Hearts. Normal trump support and 8 points.

E. ♠ K 10 x   ♡ x x   ◊ A J x   ♣ x x x x x
Three No Trump. Eight points, no good suit, and
no support for partner's suit.

F. ♠ A Q x x   ♡ x x x   ◊ K J x x   ♣ x x
Two Spades. A natural response, awaiting developments. With 10 high-card points, slam will be
reached.

OPENING NO TRUMP BIDS

ONE NO TRUMP

The point count requirement is 16 to 18.

To qualify as an opening No Trump bid a hand
must have not only the right size but the right shape.
The acceptable shapes are:

4-3-3-3   4-4-3-2   5-3-3-2

A No Trump opening should not be made with
a hand containing a worthless doubleton. A doubleton must be headed by one of the high honors. At
least three suits must be protected.

Hands which count 19, 20, or 21 are too big for one No Trump and must be opened with one of a suit.

♠ Q J 10   ♡ K x x   ◇ A x x   ♣ A K x x

Bid one No Trump. (17 points)

♠ K x x   ♡ K Q x   ◇ A x x   ♣ A K J x

Bid one Club. The hand is too big for one No Trump. (20 points)

♠ K x x   ♡ A K x   ◇ 10 x x x   ♣ A 10 x

Bid one Club. The hand is not big enough for one No Trump. (14 points)

TWO NO TRUMP

The point count requirement is 22, 23, or 24 points.

The hand must be of a balanced type.

All suits must be protected.

An opening bid of two No Trump, unlike an opening bid of two in a suit, is not forcing. If partner has nothing he may pass.

♠ A K J   ♡ K Q x   ◇ A J x   ♣ K Q 10 x

Bid two No Trump. (23 points)

♠ K Q J x x   ♡ A K J   ◇ K Q   ♣ Q J x

Bid two No Trump. (22 points)

THREE NO TRUMP

The point count requirement is 25, 26, or 27 points.

The hand must be balanced in type.

All suits must be protected.

♠ A K Q   ♡ K Q x   ◇ A K 10   ♣ K J 9 x

Bid three No Trump. (25 points)

26

RESPONSES TO NO TRUMP BIDS

Remember it takes 26 points to make game at No Trump, a little less with a good five-card suit. 33 or 34 points will normally produce 12 tricks. 37 or 38 points will normally produce 13 tricks.

RESPONSES TO ONE NO TRUMP

With a balanced hand:

Raise the No Trump if you have the required count. Do not show your suit.

Raise to two No Trump with 8 or 9 points. (Or with 7 points if you have a good five-card suit.)

Raise to three No Trump with 10 to 14 points.

Raise to four No Trump with 15 or 16 points.

Raise to six No Trump with 17 or 18 points.

If you hold 19 or 20 points, a bid of six No Trump is not quite adequate. First make a jump shift to three of some suit, and then follow up with six No Trump. Showing a suit and jumping to six No Trump is a little stronger action than just jumping to six No Trump.

Raise to seven No Trump with 21 or more, your partnership is assured of at least 37 points.

THE TWO CLUB CONVENTION

A response of two Clubs is artificial and shows a minimum of eight high-card points and a holding of at least four cards in one of the major suits. It requests opener to show a biddable four-card major (Qxxx or better) if he has one. If opener has no four-card major, he bids two Diamonds (this call is artificial and has no relation to the suit itself).

After opener's rebid, the responder must take control. With ten points or more he should make a jump bid to assure reaching a game contract. With eight or nine points he must either raise opener's major suit or return to two No Trump. If opener has denied a major suit by rebidding two Diamonds, responder must not show a four-card major of his own. In this sequence, such a call unconditionally promises a five-card suit.

In employing the convention, when responder bids two Diamonds, two Hearts or two Spades, opener is not expected to bid again so that if responder has a hand of moderate strength containing a five-card major suit, he must first bid two Clubs.

Examples:

NORTH	SOUTH
1 No Trump	?

(1) ♠ Qxxx ♡ Axxx ◇ KJxx ♣ x

(2) ♠ xxx   ♡ Kxxx ◇ AJ10x ♣ xx

(3) ♠ KQxxx ♡ Kxx ◇ xx   ♣ xxx

The correct response on each of these hands is two Clubs.

(1) If opener shows a major suit, responder will raise to four; if he bids two Diamonds, denying a major, responder will go directly to three No Trump.

(2) If opener bids two Hearts, responder will raise to four; if opener bids two Diamonds or two Spades, responder will return to two No Trump.

(3) If opener bids two Spades, responder will raise to three; if opener bids two Diamonds or two Hearts, responder will bid two Spades. This call is not forcing and opener may pass with a bare minimum.

TAKEOUT TO TWO DIAMONDS, TWO HEARTS, OR TWO SPADES

This is a sign of relative weakness and shows a five-card suit with less than eight high-card points. The No Trump bidder is requested to pass.

TAKEOUT TO THREE OF A SUIT

This shows at least a good five-card suit and 10 points or more in high cards. It is forcing to game.

TAKEOUT TO FOUR OF A SUIT

This is done on a hand containing a long suit (at least six cards in length) but less than 10 points in high cards. The hand should be able to produce about five tricks.

REBIDS BY OPENING NO TRUMPER

If partner bids two Clubs, you must show a biddable four-card major suit (Q x x x) or better if you have one. With no major bid two Diamonds. With both majors bid two Spades first.

If partner bids two of any other suit this is a request to pass. However, holding a maximum No Trump with a good trump fit, you may offer a single raise.

If partner raises your one No Trump to two, go on to game unless you have a minimum. If partner raises your one No Trump to three, pass.

If partner jumps to three in a suit you must bid again. (This is a strength-showing response.)

If partner jumps to four Spades or four Hearts, pass.

With a balanced hand:

With 4 to 8 points, raise to three No Trump. You know there is no slam, since the most partner can have is 24 points ($24+8=32$).

With 9 points, raise to four No Trump. There may be a slam if partner has a maximum of 24 points ($24+9=33$).

With 10 points, there will be a slam unless partner has a minimum (22 points). Therefore, first bid a suit and then raise to four No Trump. Bidding a suit and raising to four No Trump is stronger than just bidding four No Trump.

With 11 or 12 points, bid six No Trump. You have at least 33 points if partner has a minimum of 22 ($22+11=33$), and at most you have 36 if partner has a maximum of 24 ($24+12=36$).

With 13 or 14 points, first bid a suit and then bid six No Trump. This is stronger than just bidding six No Trump directly. It asks partner to bid seven if he has a maximum.

With 15 points, you may bid seven No Trump. No checking for Aces is necessary, for opponents cannot have one if partner has bid correctly ($22+15=37$). Opponents have at most 3 points.

With unbalanced hands:

(1) Bid any six-card major suit regardless of the high-card content of your hand.

(2) Bid any five-card major suit if your hand contains at least 4 points in high cards. (This may be shaded to 3 points with a highly unbalanced hand.)

(3) Jump to four in a major suit with a six-card suit and a hand containing about 8 points in high cards.

(4) With at least four points in high cards and a four-card major, bid three Clubs. This asks the opener to show a four-card major suit. With no biddable major, opener rebids three Diamonds.

RESPONSES TO THREE NO TRUMP

With a five-card suit and 5 points in high cards, bid that suit. With 7 points and no five-card suit, bid four No Trump. With 8 or 9 points, bid six No Trump. With 10 or 11 points, bid four Diamonds (artificial) and then six No Trump. Partner should bid seven with a maximum. With 12 points, bid seven No Trump.

RESPONSES TO ONE OF A SUIT

When your partner opens with one of a suit and the next hand passes, you should make every reasonable effort to keep the bidding alive if you can do so cheaply. If you have nothing, of course you should pass.

Even with one bare trick you should pass if you have no favorable distribution. With a point count of 6 you should make some response.

Partner opens one Spade.

♠ xxx ♡ Axxx ◇ xxx ♣ xxx (4 points)

Pass. But sometimes even with less high-card strength you should respond if you have a six-card suit that can be bid at the level of one.

♠ xx   ♡ K10xxxx   ◇ xxx   ♣ xx

If partner opens one Club, you should risk a one Heart response. But if partner opens one Spade, you should pass. This hand is worth 5 points at Hearts.

If you hold 6 points, it is your duty to keep the bidding open in some manner or other.

*On these poor hands respond with one of a suit
if that is the cheapest available bid. Respond with
one No Trump if that happens to be the cheapest
available bid.*

Remember that a response of one Diamond, one
Heart, or one Spade may be made on as little as 6
points. A response of one No Trump may also be
made on only 6 points. But if responder shows his
suit at the two level, he must have greater strength.

The one No Trump response shows an indifferent
hand, somewhere between 6 and 10 points in high
cards, but no more. Always prefer a response of one
in a suit to a response of one No Trump. Don't
respond with one No Trump if your hand contains
more than 10 points.

With support for partner's suit a single raise may
be given on hands ranging from 7 to 10 points, including high cards and distribution.

Support for partner's suit in this sense means
x x x x, Q x x or J 10 x.

If partner rebids his suit, he shows a rebiddable
five-card suit. Normal support then becomes x x x or
Q x.

If partner bids his suit three times without your
support in that suit, you may presume he has a six-
card suit. Normal support then becomes x x or Q.

DUMMY POINTS

When you contemplate raising partner your points
are counted somewhat differently. You consider (a)
high cards, (b) short suits.

34

(a) High cards are computed at their face value. But the King of partner's suit is promoted to 4 points, the Queen to 3 points, and the Jack to 2 points. However, no promotion takes place if you have already counted 4 natural points in the trump suit.

(b) Short suits:

Add 1 point for each doubleton.

Add 3 points for each singleton.

Add 5 points for a void.

Certain deductions are made when dummy contains a flaw. When raising partner

(1) Possession of only three trumps is a flaw.

(2) A dummy which is distributed 4-3-3-3 is considered to have a flaw.

Partner opens 1 Heart. You hold:

♠ xx ♡ Kxxx ◊ Qxxx ♣ xxx

This hand is worth 7 points—4 for the King of trumps, 2 for the Queen of Diamonds, and 1 for the doubleton. Bid two Hearts.

♠ xxxx ♡ Axx ◊ x ♣ KJxxx

This hand is worth 10 points. On the surface it appears to be worth 11—8 in high cards and 3 for the singleton. But the hand has only three trumps, a flaw for which a point must be deducted. It is therefore not too big for a single raise to two Hearts.

RESPONSE OF TWO IN A SUIT

If in order to show your suit it is necessary to increase the contract, your hand will have to be a little better. With a balanced hand you should have at

35

least 10 points in high cards. If your hand is highly unbalanced, you may count your distributional points to bring you above 10. When in doubt whether to bid two of a suit or one No Trump, if you have 9 or less points in high cards, prefer the response of one No Trump.

Partner opens one Heart.

♠ Kxx ♡ xx ◇ A 10xxx ♣ xxx

This hand is not strong enough for a two Diamond bid. Your proper response is the cheaper call of one No Trump. You have only 7 points in high cards.

♠ Kxx ♡ xx ◇ AQxx ♣ xxxx (9 points)

Respond one No Trump for the same reason.

♠ KJx ♡ xx ◇ AKxx ♣ xxxx (11 points)

Respond two Diamonds. You have 11 points in high cards, which makes it too strong for a one No Trump response.

TO RAISE OR NOT TO RAISE

When you must choose whether to raise partner's major suit from one to two or to show your own suit, the question is: Can you afford to do both? If you can, full speed ahead. If you cannot afford both, then it is more desirable to raise partner's major suit than to show your own suit.

You can afford to bid twice when your hand is worth 11 points (sometimes 10).

STRONG RESPONSES

DOUBLE RAISE

A jump from one to three in partner's suit by a responder who has not previously passed is forcing to game. It requires slightly better than normal trump support (including at least four trumps). *Responder should also have the equal of an opening bid,* i.e., 13 to 16 points in high cards and distribution.

♠ K J 10 9 ♡ x ◇ x x x x x ♣ A Q 10

Partner bids one Spade. Raise to three Spades. (13 points)

♠ K Q x x ♡ x x ◇ A x x x ♣ K x x

Partner bids one Spade. Raise to three Spades. (13 points)

♠ J x x ♡ K x x x ◇ A K x ♣ K J x

Partner bids one Heart. Raise to three Hearts. (15 points)

If responder's hand is considerably stronger than this, a jump to three of the opening bidder's suit is not proper. The double raise is used to make sure of getting to game, but is not the right bid when a slam can be visualized immediately.

Hands that are valued at 17 or 18 points in support of partner are not strong enough for an immediate jump shift but are nevertheless too strong for the double raise, and their strength must be described in a series of bids. Responder will obtain best results

by making simple forces in a new suit twice before
raising opener's bid.

♠ x
♡ A x x x
◇ K Q J x
♣ K Q x x

Partner bids one Heart. You have 18 points in
support and temporize with two Diamonds. If partner
rebids two Hearts you will have to temporize again
with three Clubs. Hearts will then be raised on the
next round.

Where the responder can immediately visualize
a slam after his partner's opening bid, he should make
a jump shift response. See the paragraphs on slam
bidding, pages 40–41 and 102.

RESPONSE OF TWO NO TRUMP

*A jump to two No Trump by a responder who
has not previously passed is forcing to game.* Responder must have about the equal of an opening bid,
all unbid suits protected, and at least two cards of
partner's suit. This bid requires 13 to 15 points in
high cards.

♠ 10 x   ♡ K J x x   ◇ K Q 10   ♣ A 10 9 x

Partner opens one Spade. (13 points) Respond two
No Trump.

♠ x x   ♡ A x x x   ◇ A x x   ♣ K x x x

Not strong enough for a response of two No Trump. Bid two Clubs, intending to bid two No Trump if partner's rebid is two Spades. (Only 11 points)

♠ Qxx ♡ xxx ♢ KJxx ♣ AKx

Strong enough for two No Trump, but the unbid Hearts are wide open. Bid two Diamonds and await developments.

Don't make the mistake of responding with two No Trump on hands that contain considerably more than an opening bid. Such hands have slam possibilities, and the response should either be a forcing takeout or a jump to *three* No Trump.

The maximum two No Trump response is 15 points.

RESPONSE OF THREE NO TRUMP

This response describes a hand which could have been opened with one No Trump if the responder had been the opener. In other words, a point count of 16 to 18. With a hand containing 19 some stronger response should be made. The 3 No Trump response should be made only on hands distributed 4-3-3-3.

♠ Qxx ♡ AQx ♢ Kxxx ♣ AQx

Partner opens one Spade. Respond three No Trump. (Point count of 17)

When the responder raises the opening bid to four in the same suit, he shows a hand that is rich in trump support (at least five) and distribution (it must contain a singleton or void suit)—*but that is not rich in high cards.* Such a raise should never be made on a hand which contains more than 9 points in high cards, since then it would qualify as a double raise.

The triple raise is frequently referred to as a shut-out bid. This is an improper expression. It is merely a *descriptive* bid. Who is the responder to shut out his partner? Let the responder just bid his own hand; and if all the opener needs is *trump support, a single-ton, and one high card* for a slam, then he is at perfect liberty to bid it.

Remember: *A jump from one to three indicates good trump support plus good high-card strength.*

A jump from one to four indicates better trump support but less high-card strength.

JUMP TAKEOUT IN A NEW SUIT

This bid is employed by the responder to make the immediate announcement that he is interested in a slam. If only a game contract is contemplated, responder need not make a jump shift. The mere naming of a new suit (without a jump) forces another bid from partner, and game strength may be indicated on the next round of the bidding.

The textbook requirement for a jump shift is 19 points, including high cards and distribution. Responder should, at the time of the shift, have a fairly good idea of where the hand can safely play. If you have such knowledge, you need not have support for partner's suit.

♠ A K Q 10 x ♡ x ◇ A K J x x ♣ x x

Partner opens with one Heart. Respond *two* Spades. (20 points)

♠ x ♡ A Q 10 x ◇ A K J x x ♣ x x x

Partner opens with one Spade. Respond *two* Diamonds. (Only 16 points)

♠ A Q 10 x ♡ x ◇ A K J x ♣ Q J x x

Partner opens with .one Spade. Respond *three* Diamonds. This hand is worth 20 points in support of Spades.

FORCING BIDS

Since there are many hands on which we have various things to say and cannot do so all at once, there must be some way to assure ourselves of another chance to speak. The way to do so is to make a *forcing bid;* that is, a bid which partner under no circumstances is permitted to pass.

Some bids are *forcing for only one round.* That is, partner must speak once more. Others are *forcing to game.* That is, both partners are obligated to keep bidding until game is reached, unless the opponents in the meantime have been doubled for profits.

GAME FORCES

1. *An opening bid of two in a suit is unconditionally forcing to game.* Where a part score is held by the bidding side, an opening bid of two in a suit, even though it completes the game, is forcing on responder for one round; but thereafter responder need not bid again unless opener jumps in a new suit.

For example: Opener has 60 part score and bids

43

two Spades. Responder must speak. Let us assume he responds two No Trump. Opener now bids three Clubs. Responder may pass. Game has been contracted for. But if the opener rebids *four* Clubs (a *jump* in a new suit) instead of only three Clubs, responder would be obliged to speak once more, even though game has already been reached.

Note: An opening bid of two No Trump is not forcing. If partner has nothing, he may pass.

2. *A jump bid in a new suit (after partner has made some bid) is forcing to game.*

SOUTH	WEST	NORTH	EAST
1 ◇	Pass	3 ♣	
		or 2 ♡	

SOUTH	WEST	NORTH	EAST
1 ♠	Pass	1 N T	Pass
3 ♣			

Even when a part score is held, a jump shift demands one more bid from partner.

Exception: When partner has not yet made a bid, a jump in a new suit is not completely forcing.

SOUTH	WEST	NORTH	EAST
1 ♡	1 ♠	Pass	Pass
3 ◇			

The three Diamond bid is the strongest kind of invitation, but partner is permitted to pass.

Another exception: Where partner's previous bid has been a response to a takeout double he may pass a jump in a new suit if his hand has absolutely no trick-taking possibility.

South holds

♠ xxxx   ♡ xx   ◇ xxx   ♣ Jxxx

WEST	NORTH	EAST	SOUTH
1 ♠	Double	Pass	2 ♣
Pass	3 ♡	Pass	?

South may pass. His reason is: "Game is impossible, for I am trickless." If partner had game in his own hand, he would have made a cue bid.

3. *A bid of the suit previously named by adversary (cue bid) is forcing to game.*

4. *A jump by responder (provided he has not previously passed) is forcing to game.*

OPENER	RESPONDER	*or*	OPENER	RESPONDER
1 ♠	3 ♠		1 ♠	2 N T

Neither of these bids is forcing if the person making them has previously passed, nor where part score exists.

5. *When both partners have shown great strength, all bids are forcing to game.*

OPENER	RESPONDER
1 ♠	2 ♡
2 N T	3 ♠

The three Spades is forcing to game. The opener has shown strength, and responder has shown great strength by twice increasing the contract. If responder did not have a good hand he would not have responded with two Hearts. He would merely have bid two Spades in the first place.

6. *When a player responds to a semi-force it is assumed the partnership is going to game.*

OPENER	RESPONDER	*or*	OPENER	RESPONDER
1 ♡	1 ♠		1 ♡	1 ♠
2 NT	?		3 ♡	?

Responder is permitted to pass, but if he bids again game must be reached.

Similarly, the opening bid is two No Trump. Responder bids three of a suit. The partnership is committed to game.

FORCES FOR ONE ROUND

When a major suit has been supported, the showing of any other suit is a one-round force.

OPENER	RESPONDER
1 ♠	2 ♠
3 ♢	

Responder must bid once more.

Any new suit shown by responder (provided he has not previously passed) is forcing for one round unless a part score is held and the response completes a game. But a new suit shown by opener is not forcing on the responder, who is at liberty to pass.

There are several exceptions to the new suit-forcing principle.

46

A. When responder bids immediately over an adverse double.

SOUTH	WEST	NORTH	EAST
1 ♠	Double	2 ♦	Pass
?			

South is not obliged to bid again.

B. When responder shows a *new suit, after* opener has made a rebid of one No Trump.

OPENER	RESPONDER
1 ♡	1 ♠
1 N T	2 ♣

Opener need not bid again.

C. When responder names a suit in response to an opening bid of one No Trump, this is not forcing. This does not apply to a response of two Clubs. See page 29.

REBIDS BY OPENER

Opener's second bid is his most important. It must tell what kind of hand the opening bid was made on.

It is more important to indicate the strength of your hand as a whole than to indicate where that strength lies.

♠ AKJxx ♡ Jx ◇ KQx ♣ A10x

You open one Spade. Partner responds two Hearts. You would like to show the rebiddable Spade suit, but to rebid two Spades would indicate that you had opened a mediocre hand. Therefore you rebid two No Trump, which shows a strong hand with well-distributed values.

It is more important to describe the hand than to describe the suit. A non-jump rebid of two No Trump shows at least 15 high-card points.

REBID WHEN PARTNER HAS GIVEN SINGLE RAISE

Opener must bear in mind that partner's raise may

have been very light and he should therefore not proceed unless he has definite excess values. A good practical guide is:

When partner makes a single raise of your opening bid (in the absence of competition), don't continue the bidding with less than 16 points, for partner can have only 10 at most.

Revalue your hand when partner raises your suit. *Add an additional point for the fifth trump and 2 additional points for the sixth and each subsequent trump.*

If you find that the partnership cannot possibly have 26 points, don't bid again. If there is a chance that your combined assets may reach 26, you should try once more. Remember partner's single raise shows 7 to 10 points.

You open one Spade. Partner raises to two.

A. ♠ A K x x x   ♡ A x x   ◇ Q x x   ♣ x x
B. ♠ A K x x x   ♡ A x x   ◇ K J x   ♣ x x
C. ♠ A 9 x x x x   ♡ A K   ◇ Q J 10   ♣ x x

A. Pass. Your hand had an original valuation of 14 points. Now that Spades have been supported, you add 1 point for the fifth Spade, giving you a revised value of 15 points. Game is impossible, for partner can have no more than 10.

B. Bid three Spades. Your hand is revalued at 17 points. If partner has 9 he should go on to 4.

C. Bid four Spades. Your hand had an original value of 16 points, now that Spades have been supported, re-valuation gives you a rebid value of 19 points, and you may be sure partner has 7.

50

When partner responds with one No Trump, don't expect very much. In a majority of cases game will be impossible. If you reach that conclusion, make no further bid with a hand of the No Trump family. The No Trump family of hands includes these distributions:

$$4-3-3-3$$
$$4-4-3-2$$
$$5-3-3-2$$

In other words, where game is hopeless do not rebid a five-card suit, nor should you show a second suit if you have one of the above distributions. The best place to play indifferent hands is one No Trump.

HOW TO JUDGE WHETHER GAME IS PROBABLE

This is done on a basis of simple arithmetic. Add your points to those shown by partner and keep your eye on the number 26.

A. ♠ A K J x x ♡ x x　　◇ K J x　　♣ J x x
B. ♠ A K x x ♡ x x x　　◇ A Q x x ♣ x x
C. ♠ A K x x ♡ A Q x x ◇ x x　　♣ x x x
D. ♠ A K 10 x ♡ A Q x　◇ A x x x ♣ K x
E. ♠ A K x x ♡ A Q x　◇ A 10 x x ♣ J x

A. Pass. You have only 13 points in high cards, so that even if partner has 10 there will be no game. With this balanced hand Spades should not be rebid.

51

B. Pass. Thirteen points in high cards and no possible game. With this balanced hand the second suit should not be shown. The best place to play an indifferent hand is one No Trump.

C. An exception is to be noted when a second major is held. A rebid of two Hearts is recommended to make allowance for those situations in which responder had a Heart suit which he was unable to show at the level of two.

D. Bid three No Trump. You can visualize 26 points. You have 20 points; partner has at least 6.

E. Bid two No Trump. You have 18 points. If partner has 6 or 7 he may pass; if he has 8 or more he should go on.

REBID WHEN RESPONDER BIDS ONE OF A SUIT

When responder names a new suit, opener must bid once more. At this point he must clarify the nature of his opening bid. *If the opening has been minimum, opener will indicate it by a rebid of one No Trump or a repetition of his own suit (or naming another suit without increasing the contract).*

You bid a Heart. Partner responds one Spade.

A. ♠ xx ♡ AKJx ◇ KJx ♣ Kxxx
B. ♠ xx ♡ AKJ10x ◇ Kxxx ♣ xx
C. ♠ xx ♡ AQ10xx ◇ KQJx ♣ xx

A. Rebid one No Trump. A minimum hand of the No Trump family (13 to 16 points).

B. Rebid two Hearts. A minimum hand of the suit type.

C. Rebid two Diamonds. Here you are increasing the contract without much additional strength, but it is the cheapest level at which you may rebid, since your hand is not of the No Trump family.

Whenever you make it impossible for partner to return to two of your first suit you promise a very strong hand.

♠ xx ♡ AQ10x ◇ AKJxx ♣ Ax

You open one Diamond. Partner bids one Spade. You rebid two Hearts. This makes it impossible for partner to return to two Diamonds and compels him to bid *three* if he wishes to return to your first suit. This guarantees a strong hand (about 19 points).

♠ AQ10x ♡ xx ◇ AQ10xx ♣ xx

You open one Diamond. If partner responds one Heart, you rebid one Spade, promising no additional values. But if partner responds to your Diamond bid with two Clubs, you must not bid two Spades, because that renders it impossible for partner to return to two Diamonds. Your hand is not strong enough to force the bidding to the *three* level.

RAISING PARTNER'S ONE-OVER-ONE RESPONSE

Where opener has support for partner's major suit he may raise from one to two with very little excess values. Opener should revalue his hand as though it were a dummy for his partner, and if he has at least 14 points (one over minimum) he may raise. A raise should not be made with less than 14 points unless four trumps are held.

53

You open one Diamond. Partner responds one Spade.

A. ♠ Axx ♡ xx ◇ AKJxx ♣ xxx
B. ♠ Axx ♡ x ◇ AKJxx ♣ xxxx
C. ♠ Axxx ♡ xx ◇ AKJx ♣ xxx
D. ♠ Axx ♡ xx ◇ AKxx ♣ KJxx

A. Rebid two Diamonds. You have an absolute minimum.

B. Bid two Spades. Your hand is worth 14 points in support of Spades.

C. Bid two Spades. Your hand is worth only 13 points, but it contains four trumps.

D. Bid two Spades. Your hand is worth 15 dummy points.

RAISE FROM ONE TO THREE

When opener raises his partner's takeout from one to three he should have four trumps headed by an honor, and his hand should be worth 17, 18, or 19 points in support of responder's suit. This bid is not forcing. Responder may quit if he has only 6 points.

For example:

♠ AJ10x ♡ AKJx ◇ x ♣ QJxx

You open one Club. Partner responds one Spade. Rebid three Spades. Your hand is worth 19 points.

RAISE FROM ONE TO FOUR

A raise from one to four by the opening bidder is stronger than a raise from one to three. It requires 20 or 21 points.

You bid one Diamond, and partner responds one Spade.

♠ A J x x   ♡ x x   ◇ A K J x   ♣ A Q x

Bid four Spades. It is worth 20 points.

This shows a hand well suited to No Trump play and containing 19 or 20 points.

This bid is not forcing. If partner has made a weak one-over-one, he is at liberty to pass.

Since partner may pass a jump to *two* No Trump, you should jump to *three* No Trump when your hand is strong enough. For such a jump you should hold 21 or 22 points.

You bid one Diamond. Partner responds one Spade.

A.   ♠ Q x   ♡ K J x   ◇ A K J x x   ♣ A J x
B.   ♠ x x   ♡ A x x   ◇ A K x x   ♣ A x x x
C.   ♠ Q 10   ♡ A Q 10   ◇ A K Q x   ♣ K J x x

A. Bid two No Trump. You have 19 points.

B. Bid one No Trump. You have only 15 points, which places your hand in the minimum range.

C. Bid three No Trump. You have 21 points.

JUMP REBID IN OPENER'S SUIT

OPENER	RESPONDER
1 ♡	1 ♠
3 ♡	

This shows a good six-card suit (or a solid five-card suit) and a hand that will produce seven tricks in the play, provided also the hand contains excess high-card values.

You bid one Heart. Partner responds one Spade.

A. ♠ A x ♡ A K J x x x   ◊ A x x ♣ x x
B. ♠ x   ♡ A K Q 10 x x   ◊ K J x ♣ x x x
   A. Bid three Hearts.
   B. Bid two Hearts.

Never make a jump rebid when the only excuse for doing so is the length of your suit.

JUMP REBID TO GAME

OPENER	RESPONDER
1 ♡	1 ♠
4 ♡	

This shows a hand about one trick stronger in playing strength than one that would justify a jump rebid to three Hearts. In other words, opener should be able to win between eight and nine tricks in his own hand and have excess high-card values.

♠ x ♡ A K Q J 10 x ◊ A x x ♣ K Q x

This is not a shutout bid. In fact opener can never make a shutout bid unless it is an initial pre-empt.

JUMP SHIFT BY OPENER

When opener wishes to insist upon a game he either bids it himself or makes a *jump in a new suit.* *A jump in No Trump is not forcing on the responder.*

OPENER	RESPONDER
1 ♡	1 ♠
?	

♠ J 10 9 x ♡ A K Q x x ◊ A K Q ♣ x

You open one Heart. Partner responds one Spade. A jump to three Spades would be inadequate. Partner might have nothing but five Spades to the King, and he would pass. A jump to *four* Spades would be acceptable, but a better bid is a jump to three Diamonds—forcing partner to proceed to game. You intend to support Spades next round. This will facilitate the bidding of slam if partner has a good Spade suit.

OPENER	RESPONDER
1 ♡	1 ♠
3 ♣	

♠ J x   ♡ A K Q 10 x   ◇ x   ♣ A K Q x x

In this case you intend to play the hand at game in one of your *own* suits. The jump is necessary to make sure that the bidding is not dropped before game is reached.

AFTER TAKEOUT TO TWO OF A SUIT

Any rebid by you which makes it impossible for partner to return to two of your first suit shows a strong hand.

A rebid of two No Trump shows a good hand.

♠ A Q x   ♡ A Q J x x   ◇ K J x   ♣ x x

OPENER	RESPONDER
1 ♡	2 ♣
2 N T *not* 2 ♡	

In general, a bid of two No Trump, a raise of partner's suit to three, a bid of three in a new suit, or any bid which makes it impossible for partner to return to two of your first suit, *shows a hand which is above the minimum range of opening bids.*

If you wish to sound aggressive, raise partner. If, however, you do not wish to sound very encouraging, rebid your own suit.

You bid one Spade. Partner responds two Hearts.

A. ♠ AKJxx ♥ Kxx ♦ Jxx ♣ xx
B. ♠ AKQxx ♥ Qxx ♦ Axx ♣ xx

A. Two Spades. You have very little excess values and cannot afford to raise.

B. Three Hearts. You have definite additional values and should not merely rebid your suit.

58

REBIDS BY RESPONDER

Responder's second bid is usually his most important call. Some responses give a complete description of strength or weakness in one bid. For example:

Weak: Single raise or one No Trump response.
Strong: Two or three No Trump, or a double raise.

But where responder has shown a new suit, it may be strong or it may be moderate. The next time it is responder's turn to speak, if he names still another new suit it is forcing, and a final decision by him need not yet be made. But if no new suit is being named, he must announce then and there whether he thinks there is a game in the hand.

The responder, as a rule, is the first one to recognize that there is game in the hand. **When responder's hand is equal to an opening bid, he should visualize a game if a convenient contract can be found.**

If he has a little less than an opening bid, there

may still be game if partner happens to have a little more than an opening bid. In other words, **the sum of two opening bids equals game.**

♠ Jxx ♡ AKxxx ◊ xx ♣ KJx

Partner opens one Spade. You respond two Hearts. Partner rebids two Spades. Your hand equals an opening bid. Partner has an opening bid. Since partner has a rebiddable Spade suit, Spades will be a satisfactory contract. It adds up to game. You therefore bid four Spades. Your hand is worth 13 points.

♠ Jxx ♡ AKxxx ◊ xx ♣ Qxx

Bidding has been as above. Spades are a satisfactory trump. You have a little bit less than an opening bid, but partner may have a little bit more. You therefore raise to three Spades. If he has no more than an opening bid, he passes. If he has some excess value, he goes to four. Your hand is worth 11 points.

♠ xx ♡ AKxxx ◊ Jxx ♣ KJx

Bidding has been as above. You have about an opening bid and partner has an opening bid. There is a good chance for game but no convenient contract has yet been found. You try to find one by bidding two No Trump.

♠ Qxx ♡ AQxx ◊ Kxx ♣ Q10x

Partner opens one Club. You respond one Heart. Partner rebids one No Trump, which may indicate an absolute minimum. Your hand is equal to an opening bid. You have an opening bid facing an opening bid, and No Trump is a satisfactory contract. You therefore bid three No Trump.

♠ Jxx   ♡ AKxx   ◇ Kxxx   ♣ xx

Partner opens one Club. You respond one Heart. Partner rebids one No Trump. With 11 high-card points it behooves you to make one more try, for partner may have 15 points, which would still place his hand in the minimum range. You therefore bid two No Trump. If he has only 13 points he will pass.

♠ xx   ♡ Axx   ◇ AKJxx   ♣ Jxx

Partner opens one Club. You respond one Diamond. Partner rebids one No Trump. Your proper bid is three No Trump. (Opening bid facing an opening bid—13 points.) No Trump is a satisfactory contract. Don't make the mistake of rebidding Diamonds.

RESPONDER CLARIFIES HIS RAISE

OPENER	RESPONDER
1 ♠	2 ♠
3 ♠	?

What is opener saying? He is saying, "Partner, I don't know whether you have a good raise (9 or 10 points) or a light raise (7 or 8 points). If it is a good raise, please go to game."

OPENER	RESPONDER
1 ♠	2 ♠
2 N T	?

61

What is opener saying? Exactly the same thing as above, only this time he has a more balanced hand, with distributed values.

Opener	Responder
1 ♡	2 ♡
3 ♣	?

What is opener saying? Again the same thing, only this time he has two suits.

If you merely return to three Hearts, it will mean you had a weak raise, and opener will probably quit. If you had a good raise, you must go to game on this round. The three Club bid is a one-round force.

REBID WHEN OPENER GIVES A SINGLE RAISE

Opener	Responder
1 ♡	1 ♠
2 ♠	?

If responder's hand is nearly as good as an opening bid he should go to game, because opener's raise shows a little bit more than an opening bid. Opener should be counted on for at least 14 points and may have 15 or occasionally even 16.

A. ♠ AKJxx ♡ Jxx ◊ xxx ♣ xx
B. ♠ AKQxx ♡ xxx ◊ QJx ♣ xx
C. ♠ KJ9x ♡ Jx ◊ xxx ♣ AQ10x

A. Bid three Spades. Your hand is worth 11 points.

B. Bid four Spades. You have an opening bid, and so has your partner. They should add up to game.

C. Bid three Clubs. You have 11 points in high cards and are on the threshold of a game.

OPENER	RESPONDER
1 ♠	1 N T
2 N T	?

What is opener saying? "Partner, you may have only 6 or 7 points. If that's all you have, pass; but if you have a little more (say about 8 points), take a chance on three No Trump."

RESPONDER TAKES A CHOICE OF SUITS

When opener has shown two suits it is the duty of the responder to return to that suit which is better for the partnership, even if it involves increasing the contract. A preference is sometimes indicated by passing, and the determining factor is number, not size.

For example, partner has bid Spades and Hearts and you have

♠ xxx ♡ AK

It is your duty to take partner back to Spades.

When the same length is held in each of partner's suits the practice is to prefer the suit he bid first. This has the advantage of giving partner one more chance, if that is your desire.

For example, you are responder, and hold

63

♠ Jxx ♡ Kxx ◇ Axxx ♣ xxx

OPENER	RESPONDER
1 ♠	1 N T
2 ♡	?

Actually you have no preference. The fact that your Hearts include the King does not render the suit a better trump. It is good practice to return to two Spades. You have full value for your response of one No Trump and should choose to give partner one more chance.

♠ Jx ♡ 10xx ◇ xxxx ♣ AJxx

OPENER	RESPONDER
1 ♡	1 N T
2 ♠	?

It is your duty to return to three Hearts even though you thereby increase the contract.

It is against my policy to show an early preference with a worthless doubleton.

♠ AJxxx ♡ xx ◇ xx ♣ 10xxx

Partner opens one Heart. You respond one Spade. Partner rebids two Diamonds. Since partner has been unable to jump, you may conclude there is no game. Since you have no preference and since you do not choose to give partner another chance, a pass is recommended.

RESPONDER'S DUTIES

Responder must study carefully the forcing situation. He must know when he is obliged to bid again

64

and when he may pass. Similarly he should understand whether his bids will force opener to speak again.

Responder need not bid again when he hears a new suit bid.

Responder need not bid again when partner jumps in same suit.

Responder need not bid again when partner jumps in No Trump.

But responder is forced to bid till game when partner jumps in a new suit.

If your partner opens the bidding and your hand is equal to an opening bid, there is a good chance for a game. As soon as you find out the correct spot hasten to game. If your hand is almost the equivalent of an opening bid and partner seems to be slowing down, coax him to bid again.

PARTNERSHIP LANGUAGE

It is important to be able to identify encouraging and discouraging bids.

Constant repetition of the same suit at minimum stages indicates great length of suit but not very much strength.

OPENER	RESPONDER
1 ♡	2 ♣
2 N T	3 ♣

The three Club bid means, "Partner, I have long Clubs but you may not find them useful at No Trump." For example:

♠ J x x   ♡ x x   ◇ x   ♣ K Q J 10 x x x
But if responder held

♠ x x x   ♡ x x   ◇ x x   ♣ A K Q x x x

it would be improper for him to bid three Clubs. He should bid three No Trump, because partner will find his Clubs useful at No Trump.

HOW TO ENCOURAGE

If you have a good hand when your partner opens and then rebids two No Trump, you must not merely repeat your suit. Either raise the No Trump or jump in your suit.

♠ x x   ♡ A K Q x x x   ◇ x x x   ♣ x x

OPENER	RESPONDER
1 ♠	2 ♡
2 N T	?

Bid either three No Trump or four Hearts, but definitely *not* three Hearts.

Not every repetition of your own suit is discouraging. If according to the bidding you were at perfect liberty to pass—yet you keep on with your suit—it shows a willingness to go on.

OPENER	RESPONDER
1 ♡	1 ♠
2 ♡	2 ♠

66

The opener has shown a willingness to quit. There is no occasion for responder to rebid Spades unless he still hopes to get to game or unless he is sure his suit will be safer than the opener's.

A preference bid made by a responder who has previously increased the contract should not be treated as discouraging.

OPENER	RESPONDER
1 ♠	2 ♣
2 ◇	2 ♠

Responder has shown a hand with more than 10 points.

♠ QJx   ♡ xxx   ◇ xx   ♣ AKxxx

Similarly:

OPENER	RESPONDER
1 ♡	2 ◇
2 N T	3 ♡

The three Heart bid denotes a strong hand and not a mere preference for Hearts over No Trump. If responder lacked a good hand, he would have responded two Hearts instead of two Diamonds. Three Hearts gives opener a choice of playing for game at three No Trump or four Hearts. Responder may hold such a hand as:

♠ xx   ♡ Kxx   ◇ AKJxx   ♣ xxx

OPENER	RESPONDER
1 ♡	1 ♠
3 ♡	3 ♠

67

The three Heart bid was not forcing; but when responder elected to bid again, the partnership then became committed to game. Any new bid, such as four Clubs or four Diamonds, now compels responder to speak.

Whenever a player takes partner out of a game contract to which he has voluntarily leaped, into a non-game contract, the logic of the situation dictates that he must be looking for a slam.

Opener	Responder
1 ♣	1 ♦
3 N T	4 ♦

Four diamonds is a slam try. Responder has no right to impose his will on opener who has advertised a powerhouse. He must therefore be trying to go places. With a bad hand he passes and takes a chance on three No Trump.

There are a few exceptions to the convention that a new suit shown by responder is forcing on the opening bidder.

Where the responder has bid over an adverse double, the opener need not go on.

South	West	North	East
1 ♡	Double	1 ♠	Pass
?			

South, the opener, need not bid again if he does not choose to. He knows that North does not have a powerful hand, for with a good hand North would have redoubled.

A new suit bid by the responder is not forcing after the opener has rebid one No Trump.

SOUTH	WEST	NORTH	EAST
1 ♣	Pass	1 ♠	Pass
1 NT	Pass	2 ♡	Pass
?			

South may pass if he chooses.

North should have a weak two-suited hand, such as:

    ♠ KJxxx   ♡ Qxxxx   ◊ x   ♣ xx

With a *strong* two-suiter, North should jump to three Hearts at his second turn to bid. For example, North might hold

    ♠ KQxxx   ♡ AQxxx   ◊ x   ♣ xx

Proper bidding with such a hand would be

SOUTH	WEST	NORTH	EAST
1 ♣	Pass	1 ♠	Pass
1 NT	Pass	3 ♡	

If the responder, at his second turn to bid, shows a suit higher in rank than the suit he bid first, his second bid is regarded as forcing.

SOUTH	WEST	NORTH	EAST
1 ♣	Pass	1 ◊	Pass
1 NT	Pass	2 ♠	Pass
?			

The two Spade bid is regarded as forcing.

69

Whenever your partner opens the bidding and the next hand passes, you naturally strain to keep the bidding alive. But if second hand bids, it is no longer necessary for you to strain, since partner automatically gets another chance. Therefore if you do speak, it is called a *free bid* and denotes a good hand.

A raise from one to two, which is normally a mild bid, becomes an aggressive call when made as a *free* bid.

A bid of one No Trump, which normally denotes a weak hand, becomes a distinct effort to reach game when made as a *free* bid.

In making free responses do not permit the length of your suit to be your main reason for bidding.

In making a free bid in a suit of higher rank than your partner's, be extremely cautious. You may be committing your side to a nine-trick contract.

South	West	North	East
1 ◇	1 ♠	2 ♡	

North's bid is forcing for one round of bidding. If South has no strength in Spades, he will be unable to bid two No Trump. He will have to bid *three* of some suit—even if his hand is a minimum bid. North should therefore have a strong hand.

Less strength is required if North's bid commits his side only to an eight-trick contract.

South	West	North	East
1 ◇	1 ♡	1 ♠	

Now South will be able to bid *two* of some suit. North needs a good hand, but not quite so good as in the previous situation.

North should hold something like

♠ AQJx ♡ xx ◊ Jxx ♣ Jxxx

But North should pass if his hand is

♠ Kxxxx ♡ xxx ◊ xx ♣ Qxx

When you open, and partner names a new suit, you are obliged to speak again in order to give partner one more chance. But if your right-hand opponent in the meantime interjects a bid, partner automatically gets another chance. Therefore any action by you at this point is taken as a *free bid* and guarantees additional values.

MEANINGS OF BIDDING SITUATIONS

The significance of the final bid in each sequence is indicated in the following chart:

1.
OPENER RESPONDER
1 ♠   3 ♠ ?
Game force

2.
OPENER RESPONDER
1 ♠   2 NT ?
Game force

3.

OPENER	RESPONDER
1 ♠	2 ♣ ?

One-round force

4.

OPENER	RESPONDER
Pass	1 ♠
3 ♠ ?	

Not forcing
Strongly invitational

5.

OPENER	RESPONDER
Pass	1 ♠
2 ♡ ?	

Not forcing

6.

OPENER	RESPONDER
1 ♣	1 ◇
1 ♡ ?	

Not forcing

7.

OPENER	RESPONDER
1 ♡	1 ♠
3 ♡ ?	

Semi-forcing
Strongly invitational

8.

OPENER	RESPONDER
1 ♡	1 ♠
2 NT ?	

Semi-forcing
Strongly invitational

9.

OPENER	RESPONDER
1 ♠	2 ♠
3 ◇ ?	

One-round force

10.

OPENER	RESPONDER
1 ♡	1 ♠
3 ♡	3 ♠ ?

Game force

11.

OPENER	RESPONDER
1 ♡	1 ♠
2 ♣ ?	

Not forcing

12.

OPENER	RESPONDER
1 ♠	2 ◇
2 ♠	3 ♣ ?

One-round force

13.

OPENER	RESPONDER
1 ♡	1 ♠
1 NT	2 ♣ ?

Not forcing

14.

OPENER	RESPONDER
1 NT	2 ◇ ?

Sign-off

15.

OPENER	RESPONDER
1 ♡	1 N.T
2 ♠ ?	

Showing great strength

16.

OPENER	RESPONDER
1 ♡	2 ◇
3 ♣ ?	

Forcing

17.

OPENER	RESPONDER
1 ♠	2 ♠
2 NT	3 ♠ ?

Sign-off

18.

OPENER	RESPONDER
1 ◇	1 ♠
2 ♣	2 ◇ ?

Sign-off

19.

OPENER	RESPONDER
1 ♠	2 ♡
2 ♠ ?	

Not encouraging

20.

OPENER	RESPONDER
1 ♡	1 ♠
1 NT ?	

Not encouraging

21.

OPENER	RESPONDER
1 ♠	2 ♣
2 NT ?	

Strength-showing

22.

OPENER	RESPONDER
1 ♠	2 ◇
2 ♠	3 ◇ ?

Mildly encouraging

23.

OPENER	RESPONDER
1 ♠	2 ◇
2 NT	3 ♠ ?

Game force

24.

OPENER	RESPONDER
1 ♣	1 NT?

Moderately strong hand

25.

OPENER	ADVERSARY	RESPONDER
1 ♣	1 ♡	1 NT?

Strength-showing bid

26.

OPENER	RESPONDER
1 ♣	1 ♠
1 NT	3 ♠ ?

Game force

27.

OPENER	RESPONDER
1 ♣	1 ◇
1 ♡	3 ♣ ?

Game force

OVERCALLS

An overcall is a bid made in competition with opponents who have opened the bidding. If your *partner* has opened the bidding and you bid over an adversary, your bid is known not as an overcall but as a free bid.

NORTH	EAST	SOUTH
1 ♠	2 ♣	2 ◇

East's two Club bid is an overcall.
South's two Diamond bid is a free bid.

An overcall should be based upon possession of a good suit rather than any particular number of points.

As a general rule the overcaller should have a suit which he is quite willing to have his partner lead.

♠ KQJxx   ♡ Kxx   ◇ xxx   ♣ xx

The opponents bid one club. This is a good overcall of one Spade.

The opponent bids one Spade.

♠ xxxx ♡ J9xxx ◇ AK ♣ Ax

This would be a bad overcall of two Hearts.

♠ xxx ♡ xx ◇ AQxxx ♣ Axx

This would be a bad overcall of two Diamonds.

Don't overcall at the level of two unless you can promise that you will not lose more than two trump tricks.

This type of suit is treacherous:

A Q x x x
K J x x x

This type of suit is safe:

K Q J 9 x
Q J 10 9 x

If you have come to the conclusion that you have a sound purpose in overcalling you should then inquire into the risk. You should expect to be doubled every time you overcall, and you must be prepared to face a very weak dummy.

Calculate in a common-sense manner how many tricks you may lose, and compute the damages. I don't wish to sound like an official of the O.P.A. but if you pay more than 500 points you're in bad standing. In other words, allow yourself the margin of down 3 not vulnerable and down 2 when vulnerable.

When an opponent opens and the bidding is permitted to die an early death, you may take great liberties in competing for the part score.

WEST	NORTH	EAST	SOUTH
1 ♠	Pass	Pass	?

♠ xxx ♡ KJ10xx ◊ KQx ♣ xx

You have the advantage of knowing that East is "broke." Partner therefore has at least a smattering of strength and you should contest for the part score with a bid of two Hearts. Partner must not expect too much of you in this situation.

ONE NO TRUMP OVERCALL

To overcall an adverse opening bid with a bid of one No Trump, defender should have a hand on which he could have opened with one No Trump himself had he been dealer. However, he must have the opponent's suit well stopped.

Opponent opens one Spade. You may overcall with one No Trump, holding

♠ KQx ♡ AKx ◊ AQJx ♣ 10xx

While an opening one No Trump bid shows a range of from 16 to 18 points in high cards, a one No Trump overcall may be made with as many as 19 points.

The one No Trump bid may be used as a means

77

of reopening the bidding when opponents have permitted it to die at one. In this case considerably less values are required. For example:

WEST	NORTH	EAST	SOUTH
1 ♠	Pass	Pass	?

♠ A Q   ♡ Q x x   ◇ K x x x   ♣ J x x x

You may bid one No Trump. In this situation partner should not expect you to have a normal No Trump bid.

JUMP OVERCALL

The jump overcall denotes a hand containing a good suit with little outside strength. It has the merits of describing the holding to partner in one bid, laying the groundwork for a possible sacrifice and of interfering with the opponent's bidding channels when they have the preponderance of strength.

These are the requirements:

(1.) The bid should be based on a good six-card suit.

(2.) The hand should contain a maximum of 9 high-card points concentrated principally in the bid suit.

(3.) The pre-emptive bidder should have a reasonable expectation of winning within three tricks of his contract when not vulnerable and within two tricks when vulnerable. The limit of loss therefore ought not to exceed 500 points.

For example:

Neither side is vulnerable:

EAST	SOUTH
1 ♡	?

A. ♠ x   ♡ xx ◇ xxx ♣ KQJ98xx
B. ♠ KJ10x   ♡ x   ◇ x   ♣ KJ10xxxx
C. ♠ AKQ10xx ♡ x ◇ xx ♣ AQJx

(A.) is ideal for a pre-emptive jump overcall of three Clubs, inasmuch as the loss should not exceed 500 points.

(B.) is not suitable. A jump to three Clubs might inhibit finding a Spade fit, should partner hold something in that suit. The jump overcall should be avoided on two-suited hands or whenever considerable side strength is held.

(C.) is the type of hand that was formerly used for a jump overcall when that was a strength-showing bid. The proper strategy now is to double first and then bid an appropriate number of Spades on the next round.

ACTION BY PARTNER OF OVERCALLER

There is seldom any point in raising partner's simple overcall, unless there is a chance for game. **While we strain to keep partner's opening bid alive we do not strain to keep partner's overcall alive,** because partner by merely making an overcall has denied possession of a big hand. Where you think there is chance for game you may raise.

Normal trump support for an overcall is less than that required to support an opening bid because while an opening bid may be based on a four-card suit an overcall usually is not. The overcaller's partner may presume that the overcaller has a good five-card suit, so that three small trumps are sufficient support.

You are South and hold

♠ xxx ♡ Q10 ◇ KQ9xx ♣ Kxx

Both sides vulnerable. The bidding:

SOUTH	WEST	NORTH	EAST
Pass	1 ♠	2 ♡	Pass
?			

You have a reasonable chance for game and should raise to three Hearts. Avoid the mistake of bidding three Diamonds. Partner is not obliged to respond to your three Diamond bid, because he is not the opening bidder but merely the overcaller.

Similarly, you are South, vulnerable, and hold

♠ xxx ♡ 10xx ◇ KQx ♣ AKxx

WEST	NORTH	EAST	SOUTH
1 ♠	2 ♡	Pass	?

Raise to four Hearts.

When able to support partner's major suit overcall, do not show suits of your own.

Whenever able to take overcaller directly to game do so. If you make a jump raise, overcaller may pass.

Do not rescue partner's overcall if it has not been doubled.

Do not bid No Trump after partner's overcall merely to show that you have the opponent's suit stopped. Bid No Trump only if you think there is a chance for game.

THE USUAL NO TRUMP OVERCALL

When a player makes a bid of any number of No Trump which could not possibly mean what it says, then the No Trump bid is to be construed as a take-out double in the minor suits.

For example:

WEST	NORTH	EAST	SOUTH
1 No Trump	Pass	2 Spades	?

♠ A ♡ x ◇ Q J 9 x x x ♣ K J 10 x x

If you bid three Diamonds and get doubled you won't be certain whether to stay there or try four Clubs. If you double, partner is almost certain to respond in Hearts.

You therefore bid two No Trump which cannot from a common-sense viewpoint be interpreted as a natural call, and partner is expected to respond in his longest minor suit.

It is important to emphasize that overcalls in No Trump have not lost their natural significance.

For example:

1.	EAST		SOUTH
	1 Spade		1 No Trump
2.	EAST		SOUTH
	1 Spade		2 No Trump

81

3.   EAST   SOUTH
      3 Spades   3 No Trump

These No Trump bids are all "good old-fashioned" overcalls. Number one shows 16 to 19 points; number two shows 22 to 24 points; number three shows about 8 or 9 winners. Each of these bids announces adequate protection in Spades and a desire to play No Trump.

If East opens with one spade and South holds

♠ K x x   ♡ none   ◊ K Q J 9 x   ♣ A J 10 9 x

he must plan on showing both suits himself, for a No Trump overcall, when employed immediately over an opening bid, has a natural meaning and is not a request for partner to show a minor suit.

The immediate cue bid is the strongest of all defensive bids. It is absolutely forcing to game and announces practically the equivalent of an opening demand bid. It promises the ability to win the first trick in the suit adversely bid, either with the Ace or by ruffing.

The opponent opens with one Diamond.

♠ A K Q x   ♡ K J 10 x x   ◊ None   ♣ K Q J x

On this hand you wish to demand a game, and the proper call is two Diamonds. If you make a takeout double, there is some risk that partner with strength in Diamonds may leave it in. Furthermore, you will have no assurance that partner will keep bidding until the best contract is reached.

Occasionally the cue bidder tells a small lie by making an immediate cue bid with a singleton of the adverse suit, but in that case he should have an overpowering hand.

TAKEOUT DOUBLES

A double is intended for a takeout:

A. When partner has made no bid or double (a penalty pass is equivalent to a bid).

B. The double is of one, two, or three of a suit.

C. The double was made at the doubler's first opportunity.

SOUTH	WEST	NORTH	EAST
1 ♠	Pass	1 N T	Pass
2 ♠	Double		

This is not a takeout double, as it was not made at the first opportunity.

A player who has opened the bidding with one of a suit may later make a takeout double of opponent's bid if partner has not yet been heard from. Similarly a player who has made a takeout double may repeat it if partner has remained silent.

♠ KJxx ♡ AK9x ◇ x ♣ KQxx

East	South	West	North
1 ◇	Double	2 ◇	Pass
Pass	?		

South should double again to compel partner to speak.

REQUIREMENTS FOR TAKEOUT DOUBLE

At least 13 points including distribution.

Ability to support any suit partner might bid, or a good suit of your own to fall back on in case of fire.

Always expect partner to bid your weakest suit. If his takeout in that suit would embarrass you, don't make a takeout double even though you have more than 13 points.

♠ AQxx ♡ x ◇ AJxx ♣ Axxx

If the opening bid ahead of you is one Spade, it would be unwise to double because partner will very probably bid two Hearts, which will leave you no safe escape.

Greater liberties may be taken with a takeout double if you have at least four cards in each major suit.

♠ K10xx ♡ KJxx ◇ AQxx ♣ x

The opening bid ahead of you is one Club. This is a splendid type of double. You are prepared for anything.

♠ AKJ10x ♡ Kxxx ◇ xx ♣ Ax

If the opening bid ahead of you is one Diamond, you should double. If partner responds with two Clubs, you have a reasonably safe escape to two Spades.

The takeout double announces: "I have a good hand, partner. I will tell you more about it later. Meanwhile, just answer my questionnaire."

When the opponents have permitted the bidding to die at one of a suit you may reopen by making a takeout double with less than the normal 13 points.

WEST	NORTH	EAST	SOUTH
1 ♣	Pass	Pass	?

♠ AJxx ♡ Kxxx ◊ Kxx ♣ xx

South should double.

DOUBLE OF ONE NO TRUMP

An immediate double of one No Trump is primarily for penalties, but partner of the doubler should exercise his own judgment. If his hand has little defensive value but contains a long suit, it is better policy not to stand for the double but to show the suit. However, holding 6 or 7 points, doubler's partner should pass.

RESPONSES TO TAKEOUT DOUBLE

First of all it is important to learn how to estimate your hand when partner makes a takeout double.

When partner doubles, if you have
6 points, you have a *fair* hand.

87

9 points, you have a *good* hand.

11 points, you have a *probable game*.

If you have more than 11 points, game becomes a moral certainty, provided you reach the proper contract.

Possession of a long suit will promote a fair hand to a good hand and a good hand to a probable game.

You must respond, no matter how weak your hand. The only excuse for passing is the belief that you can defeat the contract which partner has doubled. *This means you have at least three trump tricks.*

Don't be afraid to bid with a "bust" hand. Partner has promised to take care of you. Your response is not a bid in the real sense of the word, it is merely an answer to partner's question, "What is your best suit, such as it is?" In this situation your suit need not be biddable.

Where your response can be made at the level of one, a four-card major, if it is headed by a high honor, should be shown in preference to a five-card minor.

♠ xxx ♡ Qxxx ◇ x ♣ Kxxxx

Partner has doubled one Diamond. Respond one Heart.

Where responder has two suits and a good hand the higher-ranking suit should be shown first with the intention of showing the other suit on the next round.

♠ K10xx ♡ AJxx ◇ xxx ♣ xx

88

Partner doubles one Diamond. Respond one Spade, showing Hearts next round.

The response of one No Trump to partner's take-out double denotes a fairly good hand—at least 7 or 8 points.

Do not respond with one No Trump because you are in distress. Occasionally your only four-card suit will be the one doubled by partner. In that case, with a weak hand, you will be obliged to respond with your cheapest three-card suit.

♠ 10xx   ♡ Jxx   ◇ Qxxx   ♣ xxx

Partner doubles one Diamond. Do not bid one No Trump. Make the cheapest bid possible in a three-card suit—one Heart.

Where doubler's partner has a choice between No Trump and a minor suit, he should bid No Trump. Where the choice is between No Trump and a major suit, he should bid the major suit.

♠ J10xx   ♡ KJx   ◇ QJxx   ♣ xx

Partner doubles one Heart. Bid one Spade.

♠ KJxx   ♡ xx   ◇ Qxx   ♣ K109x

Partner doubles one Spade. Bid one No Trump.

When you hold 11 points or more and your partner has doubled, it is good policy to bid one more than is necessary even if your suit is weak.

♠ QJxx   ♡ AJx   ◇ xxx   ♣ KJx

Partner doubles one Diamond. Bid two Spades.

♠ QJ10   ♡ Jxx   ◇ KJx   ♣ KQxx

Partner doubles one Diamond. Bid two No Trump.

♠ xx ♡ QJ10 ◇ A10x ♣ KQJxx

Partner doubles one Spade. Bid three Clubs.

CUE BIDDING AS A RESPONSE

Occasionally the partner of the doubler has a strong enough hand to insist on game, but is not certain of the best contract. In such cases he may cue-bid the opponent's suit, even though he does not have first-round control, in order to get the doubler to select a suit.

WEST	NORTH	EAST	SOUTH
1 ◇	Double	Pass	?

♠ Kxxx ♡ Qxxx ◇ x ♣ AQxx

We recommend a cue bid of two Diamonds, since you are prepared to carry on to game in any suit partner shows.

After partner's takeout double, if next hand bids you are relieved of the obligation to respond. But if you have a fair hand (7 or more points) you may bid nevertheless.

♠ AQJx ♡ xx ◇xxxx ♣ xxx

Partner doubles one Heart. East, next hand, bids two Hearts. You may bid two Spades. (8 points)

♠KJxxxx ♡ xx ◇ J10x ♣ xx

Partner doubles one Club. Next hand bids one Heart. You may bid one Spade. (7 points)

90

An intervening redouble, just like an intervening bid, relieves doubler's partner of the obligation to respond. A pass indicates a willingness to have doubler take himself out of the redouble.

However, a bid at this point does not promise strength and is not really a free bid. A five-card suit should usually be shown, even without strength, if it can be done at the cheapest possible level.

For example, the opening bid is one Diamond, at your left. Partner doubles, and the next player redoubles. You should bid one Heart if you have five Hearts.

But when partner doubles one No Trump and next hand redoubles, a pass by you means that you are willing to play it there. With a weak hand, therefore, you should name your best suit.

Doubler should be cautious in rebidding. Remember partner was forced to speak and may have nothing. Make allowances for such a contingency.

Generally speaking, *the doubler should make it a practice on late rounds to underbid, while doubler's partner should tend to overbid.*

♠ AQxx ♡ xx ◇ A10x ♣ KJxx

You hold this hand and double one Heart. Partner responds two Diamonds. Since partner did not bid Spades and could not jump the bid, he cannot have 11 points, so you give up hope for game and pass. No other action by you would be safe.

91

When your partner's opening bid is doubled:

A. With a good hand—you redouble.

B. With a weak hand—you pass (unless you have trump support and can give partner a mild raise).

C. With a moderate hand—it is usually better to bid at once, because you may not have a chance to do so later.

$$\spadesuit \text{ x } \quad \heartsuit \text{ KQ10x } \quad \diamondsuit \text{ AQxx } \quad \clubsuit \text{ A10xx}$$

Partner's opening bid of one Spade has been doubled. You have a big hand. Redouble despite your shortness in Spades.

$$\spadesuit \text{ 10xx } \quad \heartsuit \text{ AKxxx } \quad \diamondsuit \text{ Kxx } \quad \clubsuit \text{ xx}$$

Under similar conditions you should redouble. Don't make the mistake of bidding two Hearts.

$$\spadesuit \text{ Jxxx } \quad \heartsuit \text{ x } \quad \diamondsuit \text{ xxx } \quad \clubsuit \text{ Qxxxx}$$

Bid two Spades. Your only chance to show some support. It also makes it more difficult for doubler's partner to respond.

$$\spadesuit \text{ QJxxx } \quad \heartsuit \text{ x } \quad \diamondsuit \text{ xxx } \quad \clubsuit \text{ Kxxx}$$

Bid three Spades. This does not show strength (a redouble does that). This will make it extremely difficult for doubler's partner to respond.

$$\spadesuit \text{ xx } \quad \heartsuit \text{ xxx } \quad \diamondsuit \text{ xxx } \quad \clubsuit \text{ AKJxx}$$

The bid is two Clubs. This is a moderate hand. If you do not bid now you will probably not have a chance to do so later.

92

PENALTY DOUBLES

A double is for penalties (as distinguished from a double for a takeout):

A. Whenever the doubler's partner has previously shown any sign of life, such as by bidding, doubling, or even making a penalty pass.

B. Whenever the double is of four or more of a suit.

C. Whenever the double is of a No Trump contract.

D. Whenever the doubler has had the previous opportunity to double that suit but failed to do so.

Guide No. 1

Whenever your partner opens the bidding (or in any other way shows strength, as by a takeout double) and your right-hand opponent overcalls in a suit which you wanted to bid, double for penalties.

As South you hold

♠ KJ9x ♡ J10 ◇ AJ10x ♣ xxx

93

The bidding has been

NORTH	EAST	SOUTH	WEST
1 ♡	1 ♠	?	

You should double one Spade for penalties. They are not going to make it. You are not doubling to show you have the Spades. You are doubling to increase the revenue. Even if your partner has a minimum opening bid, you should do very well.

Guide No. 2

Suppose partner opens with one of a suit and the next player overcalls with two of some other suit which you have stopped. If you were considering two No Trump, double instead, and you will score a great many more points.

♠ Jx   ♡ Axx   ◇ Q10xx   ♣ Kxxx

Your partner opens with one Spade, next hand bids two Diamonds. Double in preference to bidding two No Trump.

Guide No. 3

You can make a penalty double of a two Club or two Diamond contract more or less "on suspicion," and the fulfilled contract will not yield game. Doubling of two Spades, three Diamonds, et cetera, naturally must be sound. In fact, one trick leeway should be allowed for accident or margin of error, and such doubles should not be made unless you expect to defeat the contract two or more tricks.

Guide No. 4

Don't double the opponents if you think you can make more by going on with the bidding. *But when in doubt take sure profits.*

Guide No. 5

In calculating for a penalty double do not place too much reliance on the table of quick tricks or the number of points. Count your tricks in a common-sense manner (and you may use your fingers for the purpose).

COUNTING DEFENSIVE TRICKS FOR PENALTY DOUBLE

High cards must frequently be revalued because of information learned from the bidding. For example, A Q (which the table lists as 1½ quick tricks) may be valued at two tricks for defensive purposes if the suit has been strongly bid on your right but should be counted as only one trick if the suit has been bid on the left. Similarly a guarded King may be treated as a full trick when the suit has been strongly bid on the right but would be assigned only a slight value if the suit has been bid on the left.

Do not count more than two tricks in any one suit. If your suit is very long, do not count more than one; and if partner has vigorously supported a very long suit, do not count on winning *any* tricks in that particular suit.

When you hold four trumps against an adversary,

even though they are small ones, count 1 trick for their nuisance value.

Be quick to double when short in partner's suit. Be cautious when holding as many as four of partner's suit.

Occasionally we must desist from doubling the opponent in a close situation where it is feared our double will locate certain strength for declarer and permit him to play in a somewhat unnatural manner. Where your trump holding is Q 10 x x, for example, a double may warn the declarer of the adverse trump distribution and may suggest to him that he play that suit unnaturally.

Similarly close doubles of slams should never be made. There is not sufficient profit in them to compensate for the risk of affording declarer an occasional clue.

Occasionally in a highly competitive auction it is wise to make a doubtful double when you are quite sure that it would be disastrous for your partner to go on, which he might be tempted to do if you failed to double.

COUNTING PARTNER'S TRICKS

If partner has opened the bidding with one of a suit, you can count on him for about three tricks.

If he opens with one No Trump, you may count on him to take four tricks.

If he has made a takeout double, you may count on him to take three tricks.

When partner has overcalled or given a single raise, he should not be counted on to produce more than one trick.

When partner has made a pre-emptive bid, do not depend on him to produce any defensive tricks. Double on your *own* hand.

TAKING PARTNER OUT OF A BUSINESS DOUBLE

Webster (the cartoonist) to the contrary notwithstanding, you may and sometimes *should* take your partner out of a business double.

A. When partner will be disappointed in your hand for defensive purposes—that is, you can take fewer tricks than he expects.

B. You have a freak hand and are short in the suit doubled.

C. When you are quite confident that you can score more points by going on to game or slam.

SOUTH	WEST	NORTH	EAST
1 ♡	2 ♣	Double	Pass
?			

♠ xx   ♡ KQJ9xx   ◊ Axxx   ♣ x

Partner has made a penalty double but you should not stand for it. Partner will be disappointed in your hand defensively. You cannot win 3 tricks, which he expects.

SLAM BIDDING

ESTIMATING SLAMS

The diagnosis is more important than the treatment. That is, the estimate that the partnership has twelve or thirteen winners is much more important than learning that you have all the Aces and Kings— only to discover that you can win but ten or eleven tricks.

In the section on game bidding it was observed that *where the partnership possesses the sum total of two opening bids, game will usually result.* In other words, if both partners are satisfied with Spades as trump and each one has the equivalent of an opening bid, the hand should produce ten tricks.

If the partnership has combined assets of 33 points, in most cases you will wish to take your chances on a slam. But if you are persuaded that you have at least 34 points, then you should definitely make the slam commitment. There are various methods of determining the combined assets. Usually it is simple arithmetic. We may approach the problem from (a)

99

the standpoint of the opener, or (b) the standpoint of the responder.

If the opener makes a minimum rebid (rebid of his own suit or a rebid of one No Trump), his hand is known to be in the minimum range, which includes 13, 14, and 15 points.

For example:

SOUTH	WEST	NORTH	EAST
1 ◊	Pass	1 ♡	Pass
1 N T			
or			
2 ◊			

South has shown a hand of the value of 13, 14, or 15 points. If responder's hand is not worth 11 points he should abandon hope for game. If opener gives responder a single raise he is known to have a little more than an opening bid—14 or 15 points. If opener makes an ordinary jump rebid (in his own suit or to two No Trump), his hand is presumed to be the equivalent of about 19 points.

In such cases, responder should go to game with 7 points and should become interested in slam if he has the equivalent of an opening bid himself (13 points).

If the opener makes a jump shift (jump in a new suit), he is known to have about 22 points. Responder is forced to go to game and should become interested in slam if his hand is worth 10 points.

100

When the responder makes a jump from one Spade to two No Trump or from one Spade to three Spades, he advertises a hand that is just about the equal of an opening bid, or perhaps a little more, i.e., 13 to 16 points. Opener can therefore make a rough estimate of the combined partnership assets.

By adding his own points to those advertised by responder, he may reach the approximate total. If it does not approach the magic figure 33, then no slam is in contemplation, and opener is satisfied with game. But if it is possible that the figure 33 can be reached, opener should make some effort to find out if responder's jump was minimum or maximum.

SLAMS IN NO TRUMP

In straight No Trump bidding the estimate is much easier. It is simple arithmetic. Just add your assets to your partner's and you have the partnership total.

If partner opens one No Trump, he has 16 to 18.

If partner opens two No Trump, he has 22 to 24.

If partner opens three No Trump, he has 25, 26, or 27.

Remember the pack contains 40 points.

A combined count of 26 should produce game.

A combined count of 33 or 34 should produce small slam.

A combined count of 37 or 38 should produce grand slam.

101

If partner opens with two Spades, you may assume that he can take nine tricks in his own hand. By adding these to the total of tricks you expect to produce, you will arrive at the trick-taking capacity of the partnership.

♠ K9 ♡ AQJxx ◇ J9x ♣ xxx

Respond three Hearts to partner's opening bid of two Spades. If his rebid is three Spades, go on to six Spades. Your hand should take at least three tricks, and partner's bid announces nine tricks.

BIDS CARRYING SLAM IMPLICATIONS

1. Jump in a new suit.
An immediate jump shift by responder announces interest in a slam, inasmuch as the mere mention of a new suit by him is forcing for one round.

2. Jump from one of a suit to three No Trump.
Naturally suggests slam possibilities. But such a bid warns that responder has a 4-3-3-3 distribution and can therefore ruff nothing. It shows a point count of 16 to 18.

3. Cue Bids.
A cue bid is a bid of a suit previously named by the opposition. It shows either a void or the Ace and therefore the ability to win the first trick in that suit.

Before a cue bid is in order there must be an agreement on the trump suit either expressed or implied.

For example:

♠ — ♡ K 10 x x x ♢ A K x x ♣ Q J x x

Your partner opens with one Heart. Opponent overcalls with one Spade. You may bid two Spades, that is to say: "Partner, I control Spades. I am pleased with Hearts as trumps. I guarantee game and am looking for a slam. Tell me more."

Where there is a choice between an immediate cue bid and showing a good suit of your own, show your suit. While it is very difficult to describe a good suit late in the bidding, it is never too late to show that you have control of the adverse suit.

NORTH	EAST	SOUTH	WEST
1 ♠	2 ♣	?	

♠ K Q x x ♡ A J x x x ♢ x ♣ A Q x

You are strong enough for a jump shift to three Hearts, but a bid of only two Hearts is recommended in order to allow plenty of bidding space to show Spades, Hearts, and Clubs.

When a suit has been definitely established as the final trump, bids of other suits as a rule indicate possession of Aces (and Kings) and suggest slam ambitions.

♠ A K J x x ♡ A x x ♢ x x ♣ A x x

South (opener) bids one Spade, and North jumps to three Spades. South estimates a probable slam. Partner's response shows at least 13 points and may contain as many as 16. Opener's hand is worth 18 rebid points. If partner has a minimum raise, there will

103

be no slam. If he has a raise containing 15 or 16, the slam may be there.

South displays his interest in slam by bidding four Clubs, showing the Ace of Clubs. If North counters by bidding four Diamonds, showing the Ace of that suit, South bids four Hearts. If North should now bid five Clubs, it would designate the King.

Failure to show an Ace when there was a convenient opportunity to do so usually indicates the lack of that Ace.

♠ K 10 x x x ♡ Q J 10 ◇ x ♣ A Q x x

Presume the bidding to have been

NORTH	SOUTH
1 ♠	3 ♠
5 ♠	?

South should pass even though he has more than he needs for his three Spade bid. Partner failed to show the Ace of Hearts or Diamonds when it was convenient to do so, therefore must be presumed to lack both.

North should hold some such hand as:

♠ A Q J x x ♡ K x ◇ K Q ♣ K 10 x x

THE SINGLETON IN SLAM BIDDING

The singleton is just as important as Aces and Kings in slam bidding. The value of the singleton lies not only in the ruffing power inherent in a singleton of a side suit, but also in the *control*. The opponents can win only *one* trick in that suit.

104

When a player names three suits and includes a jump bid, he promises a singleton or void in the fourth suit.

South holds

♠ AKQxx ♡ xxx ◇ Kxx ♣ Jx

The bidding has proceeded:

SOUTH	NORTH
1 ♠	2 ◇
2 ♠	3 ♣
3 ◇	4 ♠
?	

South knows that North has a singleton Heart because he bid three suits (Diamonds, Clubs, and Spades) and also jumped the bid. North held

♠ J10x ♡ x ◇ AQJ10xx ♣ AQx

A leap beyond game, when nothing has previously been said about a suit which the opponents have bid, is a request for partner to bid a slam if he has no more than one loser in the adverse suit.

♠ KQxxx ♡ xx ◇ x ♣ KQ10xx

The bidding has proceeded:

NORTH	EAST	SOUTH	WEST
1 ♠	2 ◇	3 ♣	Pass
3 ♡	Pass	4 ♠	Pass
5 ♣	Pass	?	

South should bid six Spades. North's five Club bid, in addition to denoting the Ace, must be construed as requesting partner to bid a slam if he has only one Diamond loser. North's hand:

♠ AJxxx   ♡ AKxxx   ♢ xx   ♣ A

Similarly, in the following bidding sequence:

NORTH	SOUTH
1 ♢	1 ♡
2 ♡	3 ♣
4 ♣	4 ♡
5 ♡	?

North's five Heart bid should be construed as asking partner to bid a slam if he has no more than one loser in Spades, the unmentioned suit. South should bid six Hearts, holding

♠ x   ♡ AK10xx   ♢ xx   ♣ Q10xxx

BLACKWOOD CONVENTION

Do not attempt to use the Blackwood Convention on every slam you bid. This convention may be employed profitably on a relatively small percentage of slams and only on special types of hands.

Be sure the partnership has enough winning tricks to produce a slam before trying Blackwood. Be sure you know what the final trump is going to be before using Blackwood. In other words, first find out that you have a slam, *then* bid four No Trump.

The Blackwood Convention was not devised for the purpose of getting to slams. Its purpose is to stay out of them!

106

Either player may bid four No Trump, and no special holding is required. The responses are

> With no Ace bid five Clubs
> With one Ace bid five Diamonds
> With two Aces bid five Hearts
> With three Aces bid five Spades
> With four Aces bid five Clubs

After Aces have been shown, the four No Trump bidder may ask for Kings by bidding five No Trump. *However, the five No Trump bid must never be made unless it has been previously determined that the partnership has all four Aces.*

The responder to the five No Trump bid shows the number of Kings, exactly as he shows the number of Aces in response to the four No Trump bid.

Not every four No Trump bid is part of the convention. A suit must have been mentioned on the way up. If an opening No Trump bid is raised to four No Trump, that is simply an assist and is no part of the convention.

When Clubs are trumps, the four No Trump bidder must have at least two Aces. If he has only one and partner has only one (he must therefore respond with five Diamonds), the partnership will perforce reach six Clubs, missing two Aces.

Avoid using Blackwood when your hand contains a previously undisclosed void. Partner's Ace may be in that suit.

Avoid using Blackwood where your hand is not solid except for Aces and Kings. In those cases it is better to give *partner* a chance to use the four No Trump bid.

WEST	EAST
♠ A x x	♠ K Q J x x
♡ K x x	♡ A Q x
◊ A x x x	◊ K Q J
♣ A J x	♣ K x

After Spades have been agreed upon it would be unwise for *West* to use the four No Trump bid because after he learns that the partnership has all the Aces and all the Kings he will still be worried about small card losers. But if *East* uses the convention he can count thirteen tricks when partner shows three Aces and a King.

The four No Trump bidder is the captain of the team when he hears the response. He and he alone decides on the final contract.

There is one exception. When the bidding has shown that the partnership has all four Aces, responder may exercise his own judgment as to the final contract.

Where responder's hand contains a void, he may bid a slam directly over partner's four No Trump bid.

♠ A K x x x ♡ Q x x ◊ Q J 10 x x ♣ —

Partner has bid Hearts and supported your Diamonds. He then bids four No Trump. Your response would be five Diamonds showing one Ace. You fear partner will be discouraged from bidding a slam so you bid six Diamonds yourself.

A void does not count as an Ace in responding to a Blackwood bid.

Occasionally after a four No Trump bid an adversary will insert an overcall in order to interfere with the normal response. If you do not choose to double for a penalty, the Aces are indicated as follows:

Responder starts to count Aces from the suit in which the overcall has been made. For example: After the four No Trump bid an opponent calls five Diamonds. A pass would show no Aces, five Hearts would show one Ace, five Spades would show two Aces, five No Trump would show three Aces, and six Clubs would show all four Aces.

There is another exception which permits responder to set the final contract. When the four No Trump bidder mentions an *unbid* suit at the five level after partner's Ace-showing response, responder is forced to call five No Trump, which becomes the contract. This is done in cases where it is learned that the adversaries have two Aces but that No Trump will be the best contract.

GERBER CONVENTION

This is governed by the same principles as the Blackwood Convention except that it is used at a lower level.

A response of four Clubs over an opening bid of one, two or three No Trump is artificial and is treated in the Blackwood manner as a request for Aces. The responses are:

109

4 Diamonds .... no Aces
4 Hearts   .... 1 Ace
4 Spades   .... 2 Aces
4 No Trump .... 3 Aces
4 Diamonds .... 4 Aces

Where the four Club bidder desires information as to partner's Kings, he employs five Clubs as his asking bid. The response is made in the same fashion as above.

PART SCORE BIDDING

Possession of a part score by either side usually effects a slight modification in bidding tactics.

An opening bid of two in a suit, even though it completes the game, demands one bid from partner. After that responder may quit unless opener jumps in a new suit, which compels one more response.

Any jump in a new suit by either opener or responder, even if it completes the game, demands one more bid from partner.

The mere naming of a new suit by responder (which would ordinarily be a one-round force) is no longer forcing if a game has been reached. For example, with 60 part score opener bids one Spade, responder bids two Hearts. Opener may pass.

With an advanced part score it is the policy of responder to keep the bidding open with a little less than is normally required.

A pre-emptive bid still denotes a poor hand. In other words, with a 60 part score, if opener bids three

110

Spades he is not making a slam try by overbidding the game. He is attempting to shut out the opponents.

With a part score of 70 or 90 an opening demand bid of two in a suit may be made with one playing trick less than is normally required.

It is good practice to vary your tactics on No Trump openings when you have a part score of 60 points. It is proper to open one No Trump with such a hand as

♠ K x x   ♡ A x x   ◇ J 10 x   ♣ A Q x x

When the opponents have a part score it is good policy to open with about a point less than is normally required, where you have only four card suits.

The reason is that it will probably be necessary for you to fight against them should they open, and it is less dangerous to open light than to come in later, when you will be more exposed to a penalty double.

OPENING LEADS

LEADS AT NO TRUMP

The opening lead is not always a privilege; it is sometimes a burden. If you have an honor which is not part of a sequence, it is frequently a disadvantage to lead away from it. The most desirable lead is from the top of a sequence. If you have no sequence from which to lead, select that suit, all other things being equal, which more nearly approaches a sequence. E.g., prefer Q 10 8 2 to Q 6 3 2.

Leads from tenace positions in *short* suits are not desirable, but are proper if the suit consists of five or more cards. E.g., A Q 4 3 and K J 4 3 are not good suits from which to lead. But A Q 6 4 3 and K J 6 4 3 are.

It is rarely profitable to work on your own long suit if you have a completely hopeless hand. In such cases it is better to try to guess partner's suit and start by leading it, though you can contribute nothing in that suit yourself. This is sometimes referred to as the short-suit lead. That type of attack is employed, too,

113

on hands in which you fear to lead from almost every-
thing you have. Against a 3 N T contract, where no
suits have been mentioned, you hold

♠ K 108   ♡ J 432   ◊ A Q 104   ♣ 109

Since there is no attractive lead, many players would
select the ten of Clubs as the least of evils.

WHEN PARTNER HAS BID

In leading partner's suit, the highest card is not
always selected. Where you have any two cards or
three worthless cards of his suit, you lead the highest.
Similarly where you have two honors in sequence.
In all other cases the proper lead is a low card. The
underlined card is the proper one to lead from
partner's suit in the table which follows:

```
      A2   K2   Q2   92   654
   A62   K62   Q62   J62   A632   K632
  Q632   J632   9632   5432   96432
      QJ62   KQ62   J1062
```

When in doubt whether to lead partner's suit or
your own, give him the benefit of the doubt. Greater
consideration should be given to a suit in which
partner has overcalled than to one in which he has
opened the bidding. (He will open frequently on
weak suits, but his overcalls should be based on good
suits.)

114

(a) *If the doubler has bid a suit,* the leader is unconditionally required to lead that suit, though he have but a singleton and a good suit of his own.

(b) *If only the opening leader has named a suit,* partner's double requests him to lead that suit and not some other.

(c) *Where both partners have bid,* the leader is permitted to use his own judgment.

(d) *Where neither partner has bid,* the double *suggests* a lead of the dummy's suit, provided it has not been rebid, and provided the leader has no other good lead. But this is *not a command.*

LEADS AGAINST SUIT CONTRACTS

Under this heading perhaps the soundest procedure is first to put the quietus on that popular superstition "Never lead away from a King." It is no more risky to lead away from a King than from a Queen or a Jack; in fact I think it is much less risky. It is always a disadvantage to lead from any honor that is not part of a sequence. There is this distinction between No Trump and suit play. At suit play the lead away from an Ace is unorthodox and should be avoided except as a strategic move. If that suit must be led, the proper lead is the Ace itself.

115

When leading partner's suit the same principles are applied as against No Trump contracts. In other words, the highest of partner's suit is led only when you hold two cards or three worthless cards in his suit or a sequence.

THE SINGLETON LEAD

A singleton should not be led simply as a matter of course. When it misfires it can prove very damaging to the leader. The ideal conditions for the lead of a singleton are:

(1) A sure trump trick. This permits you to regain the lead before control of the hand is lost.

(2) Surplus trumps: holding A x, A x x, or K x x. One or two small trumps accompanying the Ace are otherwise useless; and one of the small trumps in K x x is useless because only one small card is necessary to guard the King. But when you hold K x, Q x x, or Q J x of trump, the singleton lead is not nearly so attractive because you are not at all sure that you want to trump with this holding.

(3) Partner has bid. This gives you a good chance to reach his hand in order to obtain the ruff.

Whenever you hold four or more trumps, the singleton lead is usually undesirable. A long side suit should be led in an effort to establish a force against declarer and use up his trumps.

The singleton lead is a device that should be employed on a hand that seems otherwise hopeless.

A singleton lead against a slam contract is some-

116

times effective. It succeeds whenever partner has the Ace of the suit led or the Ace of trumps.

A singleton King, unless partner has bid the suit, should almost never be led. And the singleton Queen runs it a close second as a "don't" lead.

TAKING A LOOK AT THE DUMMY

Avoid leading Aces at random. Aces were meant to capture Kings and Queens. When led, they succeed in fishing out only deuces and treys. Some players go out of their way to open with an Ace in order to have a look at the dummy. This is a rather steep price to pay for the privilege inasmuch as the very same view is available to you upon the lead of a deuce.

THE TRUMP LEAD

The advice generally given to a lady in doubt is to lead trumps. This, of course, covers a multitude of sins, because some ladies are always in doubt. Perhaps it is better policy to lead trumps when that procedure appears to be the best defense. Trump leads are indicated when it sounds from the bidding as though the dummy has a short suit.

If declarer has bid two suits and the dummy has supported only one of them, there is a good chance that dummy will be short of the other, and trump leads may prevent some ruffs.

When dummy has given a single raise and opener immediately leaped to game (showing a good hand), if you have some high-card strength you may con-

117

clude that dummy's raise was based on a short suit. Trump leads are then very effective.

When declarer has been trying to play No Trump and dummy returns to the suit, a shortage may be diagnosed; and a trump opening is indicated.

When partner has opened with No Trump and the opponents subsequently play the hand, trump leads are effective if dummy has ever raised.

A trump lead is mandatory when you have made a takeout double of a one-bid and partner has left it in.

DOUBLETON LEADS

The lead of a doubleton—merely because it is a doubleton—is not a good idea. The ideal conditions for the doubleton lead are the same as those mentioned in the discussion of singleton leads.

The doubleton is sometimes led not so much with the idea of obtaining a ruff as for the purpose of exiting when no attractive lead is available.

The lead of a doubleton containing the Queen or Jack should be avoided. These cards are too important to flip casually upon the table for public consumption.

The lead of the Ace from A x is on the whole not profitable and is commonly referred to as the "prayer lead." It should be employed only when the situation is a bit desperate.

Holding a doubleton Ace-King, and desiring a ruff, the conventional lead is first the Ace and then the King.

LEADING FROM A THREE-CARD SUIT

When you find it necessary to lead from a three-card suit headed by an honor, lead the *lowest* card, not the middle one. If your choice is between K x x and Q x x, lead from the King. That card is hardy enough to withstand an unfortunate lead, but the Queen is not.

UNDERLEADING ACES

The advice not to underlead an Ace on the opening is pretty sound for all practical purposes. An occasional surprise attack, however, may produce good results. The conditions which foster such a lead are these: The bidding suggests that the King of the suit in question will appear in dummy. You may have gathered this from the fact that dummy made a take-out double or bid strongly in No Trump. If declarer has the Jack, he will very likely play you to have led from the Queen rather than the Ace and consequently misguess the situation.

LEADS AGAINST SLAMS

The lead of an Ace with no other trick in prospect is not as a rule recommended. Remember it takes two tricks to beat a slam. Before the Ace is released an effort should be made to build up a second trick. If you have a probable trump trick it is, of course, obligatory to cash your Ace at once; or the same reasoning may be applied where you are very short of trumps and have the feeling that partner may have a trump trick.

Trump leads against slams are not on the preferred list, though they occasionally turn out well.

The singleton lead against a slam is recommended when your hand is completely worthless. Partner probably holds a trick. The hand is defeated if partner's trick is the Ace of the suit you have led; or, equally, if he happens to have a quick trump trick.

Against No Trump slams aggressive leads as a rule are not prescribed. It is wise not to lead from a holding that is likely to present declarer with a trick.

WHEN PARTNER HAS DOUBLED

Doubles of a slam by the player who does not have the lead *are for the purpose of directing leads* and not for enrichment. Against a suit slam, the double calls for the first suit bid by dummy. If dummy has bid nothing but trumps, then lead the first side suit bid by declarer. In other words, the leader is *not* to make a normal lead when partner doubles a slam.

When partner doubles a No Trump slam, the rule is not applied with quite so much strictness. Where the logic of the situation calls for it, the leader may use his own discretion.

OPENING LEAD TABLE

Holding in suit	Against No Trump	Against Trump Bids
A K Q J	A	K
A K Q x x x	A	K

120

AKQxx	K	K
AKQx	K	K
AKx	K	K
AKJ10	A	K
AKJx	K	K
AK10x	K	K
AKJxx	x	K
AKJxxxx	A	K
AKxxxx	x	K
AK109x	10	K
AK109xx	10	K
AKxxx	x	K
AQJxx	Q	A
KQJxx	K	K
KQ10xx	K	K
KQ742	4	K
QJ10xx	Q	Q
QJ9xx	Q	Q
QJ742	4	4
J109xx	J	J
J108xx	J	J
J10742	4	4
1098	10	10
10974	4	10
AQ109x	10[1]	A
AQ8742	7	A
AJ1082	J	A
A10972	10	A
KJ1072	J	J
K10972	10	10
Q10972	10	10

[1]The Queen is led when you suspect the King is in dummy.

121

Holding in suit	Against No Trump	Against Trump Bids
A J 4	4	4
A 7 4	4	A
K J 4	4[2]	4
K 7 4	4	4
Q 10 4	4	4
J 7 4	4	4
K 9 8 7	7[3]	7

[2]Unattractive lead, unless made necessary by the bidding.

[3]Do not treat the 9 8 7 as the top of an interior sequence because partner may improperly read it as the top of nothing.

TACTICS

When your choice lies between a slight overbid and a slight underbid:
  If you were the opener, underbid.
  If you were the responder, overbid.

· · · · · ·

When once you have announced a hand of great proportions, such as by opening with a two-demand bid, or by making a jump shift, let partner take charge of most of the subsequent slam activities.

· · · · · ·

Don't make doubtful decisions when you are not the last to speak. When in doubt, pass the call around to your partner. He may be in a better position to decide.

· · · · · ·

When you have previously passed, resolve all doubts in favor of the stronger of two bids. Remember that partner is apt to quit, so when in doubt raise him, to be sure the hand is played in the best suit.

· · · · · ·

123

In deciding which suit to name first, treat all very weak five-card suits (such as 9 x x x x or even J x x x x) as though they were four-card suits and bid accordingly.

．．．．．

Don't be too anxious to sacrifice when the opponents are vulnerable and you are not. By so doing you are prolonging a rubber in which the odds are 3 to 1 against your winning.

．．．．．

Though you may be more experienced than your partner, do not try to take the play of the hand away from him. An expert in the wrong contract is not so effective as a dub in the right contract.

．．．．．

If it is possible to give a complete picture of your hand in one bid, always prefer that bid to some indirect and complicated method. Sometimes there is no direct way to describe a hand in a single bid, and in that case it may take several bids for you to do so.

．．．．．

Give way to your gambling instincts when hands fit well, but bid misfits conservatively.

．．．．．

In cases of misfits, the player who can buy the hand for the cheapest price should, as a rule, be given the right of way.

．．．．．

The hand that contains the high cards will make a good dummy even though lacking partner's suit. The hand with the long suit will be a worthless dummy for his partner.

Don't try too hard to get to the best contract on hopeless hands. Any port in a storm, and an undoubled contract is better than a doubled one that may fit slightly better.

· · · · · ·

The weaker your partner the more desirable to avoid any slam conventions like Blackwood or similar four No Trump bids. Just tell him "If you think there is a slam, go ahead and bid it." This will prevent his making a stooge out of you. Instead of spending his time asking you how many Aces you have, he may decide to tell you what *he* has, in which case you can occasionally decide the fate of the hand yourself.

A DIGEST OF

THE MORE IMPORTANT LAWS

For the full enjoyment of the game it is good policy to apply the laws of contract in all their strictness. The impression is current in certain social circles that the application of the laws amounts to "playing for blood" and savors of professionalism. No doctrine could be more unsound. Even in the most friendly games certain laws are enforced, such as the penalty for revoking or leading out of turn. If other less frequent irregularities are sometimes ignored, who is to judge where the line is to be drawn? For the benefit of all concerned the rules should be uniformly applied and some of the stricter requirements should be regarded as natural hazards of the game.

NEW DEAL

If a player is dealing out of rotation or with an uncut pack, any player may, before the last card is dealt, require a new deal. But if the deal is completed, it stands.

There must be a new deal if *any* card is faced during the deal. It need not be an honor card.

There must be a new deal if one player has picked up too many cards and another too few.

RECLAIMING PACK

If during a rubber a player deals with the pack originally belonging to the opponents, the deal stands once it has begun, but at the conclusion of the hand the other side may reclaim its own pack.

THE REVOKE

There is no penalty for a revoke committed at the twelfth trick. In that case the correct card is substituted and an opponent who has played after the revoke may have his card back if he chooses.

There is no penalty for a revoke if attention to it has been called only after the cards have been mixed together. There is also no penalty if attention to the revoke has been called by the dummy, after losing his rights. Dummy loses his rights by looking into the hand of any other player.

A revoke does not become a penalty revoke until it is established. Before it is established, a revoke may be corrected (but the offender becomes subject to certain penalties for exposed card).

A penalty revoke becomes established when the offending side plays to the next trick. There is a general misconception to the effect that the revoke is established as soon as the trick is quitted. That is not the case. There is another false impression to the effect that the revoke becomes established as soon as the lead is made to the next trick. This also is not the case. The revoke is not established until one member of the guilty team plays to the next trick.

PENALTY FOR REVOKE

There is a general belief that the penalty for a revoke is uniformly two tricks. This is not true. The penalty varies. Sometimes the offender gets off without paying anything, sometimes he pays one trick and sometimes he pays two tricks.

The important point is that the revoke penalty is paid only with *guilty tricks*. All tricks taken before the revoke are regarded as innocent and are not subject to payment of the revoke penalty. After the revoke, tricks taken by the offending side are guilty tricks; and at the end of the hand only guilty tricks are used to pay the penalty. If the offending side has none, there is nothing to pay; if they have one, they pay a one-trick penalty; if they have two or more, the price is two tricks.

127

In paying the revoke penalty, there is an actual physical handing over of tricks from one side to the other, and these tricks are treated as though they were actually won in play. In other words, after the tricks are handed over in payment of the revoke penalty, you forget that there ever was a revoke and score the hand as though no irregularity had occurred.

The question is sometimes asked: If a side bids two Spades and makes two, but the opposition revokes and must pay a two-trick penalty, does this give declarer a game? Of course not. These penalty tricks are the same as those won in play. If a team bids two Spades and makes four, they receive no credit for the game.

There is no penalty for a repeated revoke in the same suit by the same player. But if that player revokes again in another suit, the same penalties apply to the second revoke as did to the first.

CORRECTED REVOKES

A declarer is permitted to correct his revoke without penalty if he discovers it in time. However, the defenders are permitted to take back any play made after declarer's revoke and change their play to that trick.

When a defender corrects a revoke, he has illegally exposed a card to his partner, and the card so played must be left on the table as a penalty card.

A declarer is never subject to a penalty for expos-

128

ing a card, for the obvious reason that such exposure can give his partner (dummy) no advantage.

INSUFFICIENT BID

If a player makes an insufficient bid, he must substitute either a sufficient bid or a pass. (A double of the previous bid may not be used to make his bid sufficient.) For example: The bidding has proceeded:

NORTH	EAST	SOUTH
1 ♡	2 ♠	2 ◇

The two Diamond bid is insufficient and attention is drawn to it. South may make his bid sufficient by bidding three Diamonds (the lowest sufficient bid in the same denomination) and in this case there is no penalty.

Or South may make his bid sufficient by calling two No Trump, three No Trump, five Diamonds, or anything higher than two Spades, in which case partner is barred from the bidding for the rest of the deal.

Or South, not wishing to bid more than two Spades, may substitute a pass, in which case his partner is barred from bidding for the rest of the deal and there is a further penalty if the offending side become defenders. Declarer may impose a lead penalty. That is to say, he may forbid the lead of a specified suit, or require the defender to lead a specified suit.

Employing the above illustration for example, South, after making his insufficient bid of two Diamonds, elects to pass instead. North is barred from the bidding and West becomes declarer at a contract of three No Trump. West may require North to make the opening lead of a Club. Or he may forbid North to lead a Diamond, or any other suit he does not wish led.

BID OUT OF TURN

The penalties for a bid out of turn (including a pass, a double, and a redouble out of turn) have been moderated considerably by the 1948 code.

If a player passes when it is his right-hand opponent's turn, he must pass when it properly comes his turn to call. (This is really no penalty at all since that is what the player intended to do anyhow.) After that the auction continues as if no irregularity had been committed.

If a player makes any other call out of rotation, the offender's partner is barred for the rest of the deal. The call out of rotation is canceled, but when it properly comes the offender's turn to call he may bid anything he likes.

SLIP OF THE TONGUE

If a player makes a call and changes it in any way, practically in the same breath, his last call replaces the first call and the act of changing the call entails no penalty. It must, however, be a slip of the tongue and not a change of the mind.

A card led out of turn becomes a penalty card. Declarer may forbid the lead of that suit, but he may not specify the suit to be led. The proper leader may lead any other suit. Declarer may at his option accept the lead out of turn and play to it as though it were a proper lead.

PENALTY CARDS

If a defender places or drops a card on the table when he has no right to do so, that card becomes a penalty card. This usually takes place when a defender drops a card, or leads when it is some other player's turn to lead.

The penalty card must be left face up on the table, and it must be played the first time its suit is led, or it must be discarded the first time the guilty player is unable to follow suit.

There is no penalty for exposing one small card during the auction. It is simply restored to the player's hand. But if a player exposes a Jack or higher card, or more than one card, the exposed card or cards must be left on the table as penalty cards.

DUMMY'S RIGHTS

The 1948 code confers upon dummy a new right; that is, the right to warn declarer if he is about to lead from the wrong hand. Dummy, of course, retains his rights to call attention to any irregularities including revokes. But dummy loses his rights if he has intentionally looked into the hand of any other player.

(The foregoing digest is based on The Laws of Contract Bridge © 1948 by the National Laws Commission.)

CONTRACT BRIDGE SCORING TABLE

Trick Points for Contractors

	UNDOUBLED	DOUBLED
Clubs or Diamonds, each	20	40
Hearts or Spades, each	30	60
No Trump { first	40	80
{ each subsequent	30	60

Redoubling doubles the trick points. 100 trick points constitute a game.

Undertrick Penalties

	NOT VULNERABLE	VULNERABLE
Undoubled, each	50	100
Doubled { first	100	200
{ each subsequent	200	300

Premiums

	NOT VULNERABLE	VULNERABLE
Overtricks		
Undoubled, each	trick value	trick value
Doubled, each	100	200
Redoubled, each	200	400
Making a doubled or redoubled contract	50	50
Slams bid and won		
Little	500	750
Grand	1000	1500
Honors in one hand		
4 Trump honors	100	
5 Trump honors or 4 Aces at No Trump	150	
Rubber bonus		
Two game	700	
Three game	500	

Unfinished Rubber—winners of one game score 300 points. If but one side has a part score in an unfinished game, it scores 50 points. Doubling and redoubling do not affect Honor, Slam, or Rubber points. Vulnerability does not affect points for Honors.

INDEX